D0616346

Praise for
Getting Back Together:

"This is an important book for everyone who is going through separation or divorce—or, for that matter, anyone in a good relationship."

—Natasha Josefowitz
Author, *Paths to Power*

"A roadmap for coping with separation and learning how to come together again after a relationship has ended. A wise and compassionate book."

—Warren Farrell, Ph.D.
Author, *Why Men Are the Way They Are*

"After you've read all the other books and are ready to go a step beyond, read this book . . . and get back together."

—Shirley Vaine
President, Women's Opportunity Convention

"A marriage is the most intimate, the most potentially rich, joyful, satisfying and productive relationship possible. This important book provides many useful insights into rescuing a relationship."

—Dr. Stephen R. Covey
Author, *The Seven Habits of Highly Effective People*

Getting Back Together

Getting Back Together

How to create a *new*, loving relationship
with your old partner and make it last!

Bettie Youngs Bilicki, Ph.D. & Masa Goetz, Ph.D.

ADAMS MEDIA CORPORATION
Holbrook, Massachusetts

Copyright ©1990, Bettie B. Youngs, Ph.D. and Masa Goetz.
All rights reserved. This book, or parts thereof, may not be reproduced
in any form, or by any means, without permission from the publisher.
Exceptions are made for brief excerpts used in published reviews.

Published by
Adams Media Corporation
260 Center Street, Holbrook, MA 02343

ISBN: 1-55850-862-7

Printed in the United States of America.

T   S   R   Q   P   O   N   M   L   K

This publication is designed to provide accurate and authoritative information
with regard to the subject matter covered. It is sold with the understanding that
the publisher is not engaged in rendering legal, accounting, or other professional
advice. If legal advice or other expert assistance is required, the services of a
competent professional person should be sought.
— From a *Declaration of Principles* jointly adopted by a
Committee of the American Bar Association
and a Committee of Publishers and Associations

This book is available at quantity discounts for bulk purchases.
For information, call 1-800-872-5627 (in Massachusetts, 781-767-8100).

Visit our home page at http://www.adamsmedia.com

Contents

Acknowledgments

Bettie and Masa: So many people have been instrumental in creating the inspiration and material for this book: the clients whose struggles and successes form the basis of this work; the couples who were interviewed, and who freely shared their experiences of separation and reunion; and the professional colleagues who offered their valuable insight and support. A heartfelt thanks to our publisher Bob Adams for his belief and support, to Brandon Toropov and Michael Selkin for their sensitivity and skillful editing work, and to Julie Castiglia and Bill Gladstone at Waterside for their warmth and friendship and for linking our thoughts and helping to bring the project to fruition.

Masa: I would like to thank my friends, especially Shirley Vaine and her daughters Joann and Michele, whose generous encouragement and support brightened my outlook during the most demanding times. My parents, though no longer with me, set an example by showing that anything is possible. That concept continues to inspire me, and has made traversing the many and diverse roads of my life possible. I am especially grateful to my sons and their wives: Matthew and Marge, Nick and Diane, and Mike and "P.J.", for stimulating my thinking, believing in me, and supporting my efforts over the years. Their faith and confidence continues to buoy me.

Bettie: No book of mine is ever complete until I acknowledge the love of my life—my teenage daughter, Jennifer. Her friendship and unconditional love are always a gift; her support and delightful energy during the hours of work needed during a project like this were extraordinary. She is sixteen as of this writing, her perspective clear, her observations on target, her approach uncomplicated. If only adults could find such simplicity in relationship dilemmas! I'm grateful for my loving parents, Everett and Arlene Burres, who lead by example and epitomize both the joys and strengths of a committed lifetime relationship. I extend a heartfelt thanks to Fran and Peter Bilicki, Sr. for their loving and supportive hearts, and to the many friends who showed integrity to our friendship when I needed emotional support, especially Ken and Karen Druck, Dale Haloway, and Barbara Tracy. And, finally, my gratitude goes to Pete—who set this book's wheels in motion in the first place.

Introduction

- Have you just left a relationship that you hoped would go on forever?

- Have you just been left by someone who vowed to love you "for better or for worse"?

- Are you living together but afraid that a separation is inevitable?

- Have you divorced—but want to get back together?

- Are you wondering whether you *can* get back together and develop a warm, loving relationship that really works?

- Are you feeling guilty for wanting to go back into a relationship that caused so much pain?

- Do you feel that there must be something wrong with you because you continue to live in the past, while everyone is encouraging you to "get on with your life"?

- Do you worry that, if you do get back together with your partner, you will be making the same mistake again?

These are probably just a few of the many concerns you have right now. Chances are, you're going through an emotionally debilitating time, a time when your heart and your mind may be telling you completely different things. You know your relationship is in more pieces than Humpty Dumpty, yet you hope it can be put together again.

Unlikely as it may seem to you right now, the fact that you are separated doesn't mean you will never get back together with the person you love. Separation is much more common than you might think. In fact, over eighty percent of all couples separate for two months or longer during their marriage. Of course, some separate permanently or divorce. But separation does not have to lead to divorce.

Many of those couples who separated are getting back together and renewing their relationship; they made the choice to enter counseling or work toward solving their problems on their own when they saw that their relationship seemed in danger of breaking apart. In some cases, there is not much improvement; the couples settle for things remaining much the same as they were. In other cases, change is dramatic—the relationship is much better than before. Some couples, in fact, are able to create a mutually loving relationship that nourishes and sustains both partners. What do these couples know that you don't? What have these couples done that you can learn from?

Until now, the stories behind these relationships have been largely ignored, but we felt it was important to make them known because of the unique insight they give us into what makes reconciliation possible. This is not to say that all marriages can or should be put back together. Some are destructive, with little likelihood of change, and such marriages may need to end.

Each of the couples we worked with or interviewed had struggled in a relationship that became increasingly painful or dysfunctional. Yet when the partners parted and built separate lives, they found that the growth made possible by their independence enabled them to join together again in a more satisfying way. These couples, who made essential changes within themselves and then reunited, show us what vital ingredients are necessary for a healthy relationship, how to keep a relationship alive, and how to mend a broken one. By listening to partners whose relationships were so painful that they felt forced into separation, who built successful new lives for themselves, and who then rediscovered the person they had once loved, we found a model of hope for others.

If you believe that there is a future for yourself and your partner, if you want to build a relationship that will nourish both of you, and if you are willing to take the steps to achieve your goal, then this book is for you.

You will be shown *how* to make a separation work for the relationship rather than against it; how to increase your sense of identity and self-worth so that the relationship has a stronger foundation; and how to go through the steps of discovery and renewal to a successful reconciliation. With specific strategies and easy-to-understand principles that you can apply right away, *Getting Back Together* helps you take the steps that can lead you back into a warm, loving, lifetime relationship.

Sometimes, what looks like the end is really an opportunity for another beginning. Divorce or separation may force you into personal growth that can lead to a reconciliation—and a much stronger, more committed relationship.

Please note that throughout this book, we have alternated the use of "he" or "she" for ease in reading, although the situations and principles apply equally to both men and women.

CHAPTER ONE

The Secret to Getting Back Together:
It's Not What You Think It Is!

- Has the person who promised always to "love and cherish" you left?

- Have you left a relationship you had hoped would last forever?

- Do you wish you could get back together again and develop a warm, loving relationship that really works?

What you thought would last forever seems to be ending. "I love you" has faded away, replaced by tears and recriminations. You remember the love you shared, the familiar routine that was your day-to-day life, your goals and dreams, and you wonder whether you'll ever be able to put them back together again. The barriers look enormous; the odds seem to be against you. Right now, you probably feel that your relationship is so damaged, so lifeless, that it's hard to see how it can be revitalized. You may be dwelling on all the obstacles. You're the only one who wants to get back together; he says it's over and doesn't even want to talk about it; you're wondering if it's possible to rekindle lost love.

Take heart. It *is* possible to rebuild a broken relationship and make it stronger and more nurturing than it was before. As long as there is still a core of loving and caring, you can start working on building the bridge to create a new and lasting relationship with the person you love. You *can* create a relationship that works for both of you.

Separation: The First Step to Getting Back Together

Are you separated, or afraid that separation is inevitable? As difficult as it is to believe right now, being apart for a while might actually be the best thing that could happen to your relationship. Time apart gives you a chance to step back and gain insight about what's wrong between you. Removed from the old struggles that caused so much pain, you can now take a time out to rest and recuperate. Because your break allows you to get to know *you* and decide what *you* want from the relationship, it can be a very constructive period. It can be a time of renewal in which needed changes can be made and problems resolved. Painful though it is, separation can be the first step to getting back together again— *truly* back together, not just physically under the same roof, but together emotionally and spiritually. It can serve as a time for dissolving destructive old patterns of relating that don't work and for learning new ones that do. This is an opportunity for both partners to grow, to restore themselves, and to come back together more deeply committed than ever.

Both partners? Chances are, right now you're the only one making an effort to salvage this relationship, and you feel quite alone. That's okay, because there's much to do that you must do alone. In this book you'll learn the steps that can help you do things on your own and strengthen you as a person, so that, eventually, a new relationship between you and your partner can take place.

Couples Do Separate and Get Back Together Again

Here's a surprising fact: more than 80% of all married couples separate for two months or longer sometime during their marriage. And nearly 18% of all couples who actually divorce remarry each other. It takes quite a lot to sever a longterm love. Marriage counselors know that nearly two-thirds of all divorced couples would choose to remain married to each other, if only they could resolve the primary difficulties that led to the breakup. Margo and Ed are typical of couples who do manage to use separation as a constructive period and to resolve their major difficulties during their time apart.

"Ed was everything I was looking for," Margo said. "Even though he said he didn't want to get married again or have any more children, I still wanted to spend my life with him. Though I always wanted children, I loved him so much I told myself that just living together was okay. What I didn't realize at the time was that I might change my mind and want to have children of my own. When I brought it up to Ed, he said 'no' right away. At first I thought I could handle it, but after a while I began to resent him for not wanting to marry me. I could see he would be a good father; he certainly was to his two sons.

"I was raised to believe that you fell in love, got married, and had a family. That's just what you did—marriage and family were what life was all about. Every time I saw my mother and sisters, they would ask when Ed and I were going to get married. They'd tell me that if Ed really loved me, he would marry me. I'd go back home to Ed feeling depressed and unlovable, doubting if he really cared. We used to have terrible fights every time I got back from seeing my family. Finally, one Sunday night after Ed had spent most of the weekend with his children and I felt very ignored, I told him I was moving out. I said I wanted someone who loved me enough to want to marry me and be the father of my children. I was hoping Ed would stop me—I gave him every chance—but he just repeated that he had told me from the start that marriage and more children were out of the question. I was heartbroken when he turned away and said, 'Maybe it would be best if we separated.'

"The separation was really hard. It lasted five long months. But it took that time apart for both of us to discover how much we really meant to each other, and to start opening up about our needs and anxieties. Ed had real fears about the possibility of another failed marriage. He had gone through so much turmoil with the ending of the first one that he didn't want to take the chance of going through that much pain again. He talked a lot about the problems the divorce had caused his children and said he didn't want the responsibility of another child who might be hurt. I could understand that, but I knew that I couldn't live with Ed, no matter how much he said he loved me, unless we were married. I needed that final proof of love. As we kept talking

about our fears and what we needed, we were able to resolve the
issues that were tearing us apart. We've decided to get married,
but we'll hold off on making a decision about having children.
Ed and I love each other, and that feels okay for me right now."

Separation Is a Symptom, Not a Cause

Unfortunately, when couples separate, one or both partners too
often focus on the separation as the problem and rush back into
the relationship, ignoring the underlying causes that led to the
breakup. Unless the focus is directed to the causes, being back
together won't change things. Separation is not the cause of the
problems you and your partner have; it's the symptom of them.

> Pat and Martin constantly argued about Martin's drinking
> and about his spending money irresponsibly. Pat threatened to
> divorce a number of times, but always gave in to Martin's tearful
> pleadings for "just one more chance." After the third separation,
> Pat knew that things would have to change before she could go
> back. This time, as Pat saw Martin's tears and heard his promises
> to stop drinking and straighten out the problems with his
> creditors if she would come back, she refused to give in. Even
> though she wanted to be with Martin and help him, she knew
> that he had to work out his problems himself. Without Pat to lean
> on, Martin was forced to face his problems and find solutions on
> his own. By confronting hard issues and working through them,
> he discovered strengths that made him feel better about himself
> and enabled him to re-design his life. Two years later, they are
> together again, this time in a relationship that works for both of
> them.

Separation Should Be Used as a Time for Making Change

Another common mistake of troubled couples is to try to get back
together *too soon*. The couples hope that if they can "get together
and try harder," things will work out. This is understandable.
Loneliness and fear of facing the future alone can lead one or both

partners to want to reconcile as soon as possible. But if you concentrate solely on getting back together, the deeper changes that could take place while you're apart, changes that could lead to a more satisfying relationship, usually don't get a chance to happen. Although you may reunite quickly, the original problems will still be there and continue to cause difficulties. The cycle may begin again, with another separation and another quick reconciliation—or, if the underlying problems are not addressed, a second, permanent separation. That's what happened to Irene and George.

> "No one ever made me feel as good as Irene," George said about their two-year marriage that had recently collapsed. "She was fun, she was smart, and she could be more loving than anyone I've ever known. But she just never understood that I needed some time to myself. Our separation was meant to be a time of being completely alone for a while. But Irene promised things would be different, that she wouldn't demand so much of my time, so we began seeing each other immediately. Unfortunately, nothing had changed. She would call first thing in the morning, put notes under my windshield wiper, call to ask about my day, and call again to say good night. Even when I said I had to go to a meeting, Irene would want to come along 'for the ride.' I felt really crowded, but when I tried to back away from her and get some space for myself, she would get angry and accuse me of not caring. Sometimes she would appear on my doorstep and cause such a scene that I would agree to see her just to calm her down. Eventually, I broke up with her permanently. I miss the good times we had, but I definitely don't miss the pressures and the crowding."

This is an example of how focusing on getting back together too soon, rather than on resolving root issues, can cause a permanent separation. George and Irene had the makings of a good relationship: They had many shared interests, enjoyed each other's company, valued the same things, laughed together, and had a satisfying sex life. If Irene had used the separation as a time to see George's pulling away as a danger signal, and if she had looked at what the real problems were—her extreme need for closeness and her fear of abandonment—she might have mended their relationship. If she had worked on resolving those issues rather than ending their separation, which only intensified her pressure on George, she could have avoided what she dreaded most— losing him entirely.

Separation as a "Time Out"

Accounts of couples who have successfuly reunited show that separation can be thought of as a "time out." It gives each partner the time and space to work on the personal problems that led to the breakup. Just as important, separation gives the severed relationship a respite, a break from constantly being tested by stressful situations just when the relationship is the weakest. It can be a much needed time of rest and healing. Physical distancing allows the old angers and hurts that get in the way of communication to dissipate while change is taking place. It gives you the chance to stand back and evaluate the strength of the relationship and in what ways it does and does not work for *you*. Just as important, it gives you the opportunity to rebuild your confidence so that you can bring a renewed and revitalized sense of yourself to the relationship. It makes getting back with your partner possible.

Although separation is deeply painful, this last-resort effort is an opportunity to work out your differences and come together in a more deeply committed relationship. The reunited couples who were interviewed for this book say that the quality of their current relationship is due to the opportunity for self-development that separation provided. While they would have preferred to work out problems within the marriage, having a "time out" gave them an impetus for growth and change. When asked, "What do you wish you had done differently?" the most common response was, "We wouldn't have gotten back together so quickly." The couples also agreed that the level of commitment and caring they have with each other now was made possible largely by their growth during the separation.

Key Ingredients of a Successful Reconciliation

Separation doesn't have to mean the end of your relationship. Many couples separate and then come back together in mutually satisfying relationships. But reconciliation, like all desirable goals, requires work and commitment. It takes clear thinking to accept the separation as a needed break from seemingly irreconcilable conflict, to understand its causes, and to begin the hard work of resolving the problems that caused it. It takes patience and dedication to create a *successful* reconciliation. Our goal in this book is to help you use this time of separation constructively, so that you can come back together in a relationship that is satisfying for both of you. In the following chapters, we'll give you specific suggestions on the work that lies ahead. Briefly, here's a preview of the key principles:

- Take care of yourself, emotionally and physically. Put the focus on you and nurture yourself in order to develop physical and psychological strength.

- Get to know and be comfortable with you. Find out who you are and what you want, at this stage in your life. Only then can you be with someone else in a mutually satisfying relationship. Take an inventory of your values and goals to help learn more about YOU.

- Develop an identity of your own. Find your own meaning in life rather than living life through someone else. Develop a lifestyle that includes your values, your needs, your talents, your contributions.

- Have a strategy for your reunion. Have a plan for getting your partner back and for creating a better relationship than you had before. Commit yourself to your plan of action and visualize a successful outcome.

- Know that there will be times when the plan doesn't seem to be working, when you will have to hang in there or modify your plan. Build a support network that roots for you and can support you in good times and bad.

- Communication is the key to intimacy. Learn to communicate in a way that nourishes a loving relationship. Learn to listen so that your partner will talk, and talk so that your partner will listen. Beneath the anger and resentment, the desire to retaliate, or the need to protect is a core of truth which is vital to changing and strengthening the relationship.

- Being back together is not the end, but a new opportunity to be with the person you love. Anticipate that there will be ups and downs in the reconciliation, and learn in advance how to deal with them effectively.

- Sustaining a great relationship takes work, too. Once you're back in the relationship, use your new skills, the ingredients of a lasting relationship, to continue to strengthen and deepen your friendship and love.

The ending of a relationship, no matter how bad things have been, is a time of regret and self-questioning: Where did I go wrong? Was all this my fault? How can I keep from making the same mistakes again? Will I ever find someone to love me again? Did I do the right thing by separating? Remember, it is possible to create a relationship filled with love, warmth, trust, and intimacy with the same partner. It won't be the old relationship that didn't work, but a new one, one that *could work*. Of course, it's not always possible to turn a dysfunctional relationship into a good one. But if there's still caring underneath the pain and disappointment, and if you want to reconstruct a relationship with the person whom you still love, know that love *can* be rekindled and that the pieces can be put back together again. The first step is to look at why the relationship fell apart—looking beyond the symptoms to the problems underneath.

CHAPTER TWO

Why Just Getting Back With Your Partner Isn't Enough:

Dangers of a Premature Reunion

During the initial painful shock of separation, it seems that if you could just be together and try again, everything would be all right. "I know if I could just talk to Julie, we'd be able to work things out. But how can I convince her that she should give us another chance when she won't see me or take my calls?" Tom's voice was filled with anxiety and frustration. He had been calling Julie for days, leaving message after message on her answering machine, but she never called back. As Tom tried to cope with his pain, he was obsessed by one thought: "If only we could get back together, things would work out, somehow."

In those first few days and weeks of separation, you keep thinking that if you and your partner could just be together again, everything would be all right. You tell yourself, "If he comes back, I'll make sure that things are different." "I'll spend more time with him." "I won't lose my temper, or be so demanding." "I'll cut down on my drinking." "I'll do whatever it takes to get her back!" "This pain and hurt will stop; my life will be normal again." Your determination and resolution are strong and sincere. Unfortunately, they're not enough. It takes more than good intentions to make your relationship healthy. There's much work to be done. It's helpful to know *why* the relationship fell apart.

The Influence of Negative History and Dysfunctional Patterns of Behavior

Two of the chief sabotagers of a successful reunion are negative history and dysfunctional patterns of behavior. Negative history is the accumulation of all the destructive events that have happened to the two of you as a couple. It's the emotional baggage you carry around with you. Dysfunctional patterns of behavior are those that trigger destructive emotional responses and create hurt and pain for you and your partner. When each partner is dealing with the worst in the other, it's hard to resolve issues and make a fresh start.

Relationships are very fragile, as you've found out. A healthy relationship requires constant care and feeding in order to stay that way. Destructive ways of interacting and the accumulation of hurts can gradually destroy any relationship. Your relationship slowly erodes under the weight of negative history. Painful memories of all the hurtful things that have happened between you—the broken promises, the infidelities, the fights—are easily triggered by a look, a word, or an action. In addition, destructive patterns of behavior—the fixed, dysfunctional ways you and your partner interact—contribute to undermining the relationship.

Remember the times you vowed you would handle things differently, but couldn't stop reacting to your partner in the same negative ways? "I know better," you say, "but he pushes my buttons." That's exactly right. When you've lived with someone long enough, you both know all the buttons to push. Even seemingly harmless actions or remarks can trigger the old, destructive emotions and ways of interacting. When he's a few minutes late, you flash back to the time he missed an important event because he never bothered to call. When he lowers his voice on the phone, you recall his old girlfriend who suddenly started calling because she had just gotten a divorce. A look is interpreted as impatience, a tone of voice that means your partner is getting angry, put-downs, manipulation. All these destructive past memories, if not dealt with, destroy any possibility of a resoultion. This can be seen most clearly in couples who reunite prematurely and don't allow time for negative memories to fade and more positive experiences to build up.

That's *why* just getting your partner back isn't enough. You've probably heard someone say, "Oh, yes, we tried getting back together, but it just didn't work out."

The Dangers of Rushing into Reconciliation

Do you want to reunite temporarily or permanently? When you first get back together after a separation, things may seem wonderful, even better than ever. You're in a kind of "honeymoon" stage, with all the excitement, warmth, and passion of a new romance. But, eventually, the old problems and old habits of interacting begin to creep back—if you haven't made some fundamental changes in the way you think about yourself, your partner, and the relationship.

When couples in troubled relationships reunite prematurely, they usually go through a four-stage cycle that leads to a temporary reunion—and eventually, a permanent ending of the relationship. It works something like this:

A Temporary Reunion vs. a Permanent Reunion: The Four-Stage Cycle

Premature Reconcilation

Stage
One: Disintegration. The problems of the relationship seem overwhelming. The negative history and dysfunctional behavior accumulate. Anger, resentment, and destructive actions escalate, leading to increasingly bitter arguments or emotional withdrawal. Attempts to deal with the problems are ineffectual. Though there is love and caring beneath the pain and confusion, separation seems the only solution.

Stage
Two: *Separation.* One or both partners distance themselves
        from the relationship (emotionally and/or physically),
        deciding the problems are too much to overcome. They
        separate and wonder what went wrong, wishing they
        could work things out, believing that if only the other
        would change, or some compromises be made, all
        would be well. The real problems and underlying
        causes are pushed into the background, and little if any
        attempt is made to understand or resolve them.

Stage
Three: *Premature Reunion.* Separation and loss of a partner is
        extremely painful. The most obvious cure is to promise
        to do better, to "try harder this time," and to come back
        together as quickly as possible. But the problems are just
        as overwhelming the second time around. If underlying
        problems haven't been addressed, and effective solu-
        tions found, the same dysfunctional patterns of be-
        havior quickly return. The couple comes back together,
        but little if anything has been resolved. The same cycle
        of problems that led to the first separation is repeated.
        The resentment and withdrawal intensify, and often the
        only solution seems to be a *permanent* separation.

Stage
Four: *Permanent Separation or Divorce.* One or both partners are
        convinced that everything possible has been done to
        give the relationship a chance to survive. After all, they
        have already tried reconciliation. They've "tried har-
        der" in the ways they knew how. Since things just didn't
        work out, one or both people feel they have no choice
        but to end the relationship.

It doesn't have to be this way. There is a model that can lead to a
successful and permanent reconciliation.

Successful Reconciliation

Stage
One: *Disintegration.* The problems of the relationship seem overwhelming. The negative history and dysfunctional behavior accumulate. Anger, resentment, and destructive actions escalate, leading to increasingly bitter arguments or emotional withdrawal. Attempts to deal with the problems are ineffectual. Though there is love and caring beneath the pain and confusion, separation seems the only solution.

Stage
Two: *Separation.* One or both partners distance themselves from the relationship. Separation is seen as a necessary step, a time apart which allows both partners space to grow, and as an opportunity to create a new relationship. Rather than attempting to solve problems by changing the other partner, the focus is on individual self-discovery and growth. New patterns of behavior and new ways of relating that can lead to a strong and mutually satisfying relationship are acquired.

Stage
Three: *Preparation.* Because of the perspective gained in Stage Two, and in the process of working toward clarifying unresolved personal issues, each partner perceives the other in more positive ways. There is no longer a feeling of desperation. Communication has improved, and both partners begin talking, openly and honestly, about fundamental issues. They see each other as desirable once more and start talking seriously about reconciliation.

Stage
Four: *Successful Reconciliation.* Both partners have grown and matured in being able to care for each other and the relationship. They have created a *mutual interdependence*. Each has learned more about himself, and about what it takes to be in a mutually satisfying relation-

ship—in particular, *this* relationship. Both partners have a better understanding of how to love and live together in ways that work well for both. They have created a new relationship that works for both of them.

The first step in the cycle of a successful reconciliation is to understand the positive role that a separation can play.

How Healing Starts

One of the major benefits of the separation stage is the time and space apart for old hurts to heal. You need time apart so that negative memories and interactions are not constantly triggered. During the early stages of the separation, if you constantly talk to each other or see each other, it's likely that you're still having the same arguments in the same destructive ways. You need a period of respite to recover from the bitterness and pain, and to begin to let go of the hurt. As you do so, and as you learn new ways to get your needs met, the old patterns can start to be replaced by new ones that work *for* the relationship. For example, if you were overly dependent on your partner for companionship, but have started to develop new interests and friends, you have something new to bring to the relationship that adds vitality.

> When Tom realized that he intimidated Julie by his confrontive communication style, he knew he needed to try a different approach. He sent her a card that expressed exactly what he wanted to say, and wrote a simple note on it, saying he cared for her deeply and hoped she was well. He didn't call for several days except to leave a message telling her about his new assignment at work and asking her about her job. Over the next few weeks, he sent two more cards, letting her know he cared, but without demanding any action in return. Finally, one day he called Julie and she answered the phone. He didn't ask for anything—he just told Julie that he was there for her, and that the only thing he wanted was her happiness.

Tom was establishing a new way of communicating, one that would make Julie more comfortable with him and create a new cycle of positive interactions. Together with the other new behaviors and ways of thinking he acquired, it would form the basis for their eventual reconciliation. That's one of the major benefits of focusing on you. When your attention is turned inward, toward the things you can do something about, your frustration and dissolution decrease. You begin to achieve perspective on your relationship—and you take one of the first steps toward a successful reconciliation.

Why You Need Time Apart

In the last chapter, we examined why separation may actually benefit a troubled relationship. It's natural to hope that "she'll come back, and things will be the way they used to be." But you're probably thinking of the way they "used to be" when you were in the first glow of the relationship, not how they were when you left. What you really want is to be together with your partner in a relationship that's much better than it was. That's why it's important to use your time apart constructively.

When you separate, you're forced to deal with fundamental issues about yourself, your partner, and the relationship itself. At first, these issues can feel so frightening or overwhelming that your first instinct is to run back to the seeming safety of the old relationship. When the pain of separation engulfs you, it's easy to forget the anger, hurt, resentment, and other negative feelings you had. Fear of losing your partner forever, being lonely, of never finding someone else to love, or of not being able to make it financially on your own can lead you to rush back to a relationship prematurely. But if the relationship is to have a chance, you need distance, a chance to step back and look at things from a more realistic perspective, and time, however long it takes, to begin to identify and work toward solving some of the bigger problems.

You also need time to regain your emotional equilibrium and start to heal, time to get to know you and discover what you want. You need time to sort through the reasons for the breakup. If you sweep the problems under the rug and decide to ignore them, they will resurface. But if you take the time to get to know yourself and your needs, and to build upon your strengths, you have a much better chance of attracting and drawing your partner back and of keeping him. You need time to love your way back into the relationship.

What Really Went Wrong in the Relationship?

In addition to mending yourself and regaining a healthy sense of self, it's important to uncover what really went wrong, to identify the underlying causes that led to the separation. Too often we see the problems as being the other partner's (awful) attitude or behavior ("How could he be so mean! He . . ."). Indeed, that is usually what one partner wants to talk about during the first few weeks or months of counseling! We remember painful events, conflicts, irritating characteristics, and disappointments in the relationship. But these are mostly symptoms of more basic problems. Concentrating on fixing the symptoms, rather than on finding and resolving the basic causes, can lead to a downward spiral of dysfunctional behavior and destructive reactions. Underlying causes of relationship problems can be as different as couples are. However, we have found that many of them can be generalized into one or more of the following categories.

Unfulfilled Expectations. Everyone enters into a relationship with an idea of what it "should" be like, especially the belief that being in a relationship will magically create happiness and fullfillment. You've probably said or thought some of these yourself: "If you loved me, you'd want to make me happy," "If you loved me, you'd know what I want," and perhaps the most common, "If you loved me, I wouldn't have to ask for what I want."

Other expectations center around male and female roles, who takes which responsibility for child rearing or home maintenance, who decides how the money is spent, who is responsible for social obligations, who upholds the standard of living. The list of expectations is endless and is based on childhood experiences in our own families as well as other influences, such as from advertising and the media. These are the experiences that define for us what is "right" or "normal." A good example is opening Christmas presents. Does your family exchange and open them on Christmas Eve, or on Christmas morning? Chances are, whatever feels "right" to you is what your family did when you were growing up. Big things, little things. We all have a belief in how they should be done. Do you squeeze the toothpaste from the top or the bottom? Do you discipline the children with spanking or not? Do you talk problems through immediately (not going to sleep on your anger), or ignore them and hope they'll work themselves out? Chances are, your way feels "right" to you, and doing things differently makes you uncomfortable—it just doesn't feel right.

Most expectations seem harmless enough. After all, arguing over squeezing toothpaste tubes seems more appropriate for a sitcom than for a marriage, doesn't it? But expectations lead to hurt, or disappointment when they are not met. At those times, it's easy to start an internal conversation ("I've told him a million times to put the cap back on the toothpaste—he's doing this just to bug me") that triggers more anger about your partner's actions and intentions.

Inability to Communicate. When communication breaks down, your relationship is headed for danger. And when the relationship has broken apart, communicating effectively becomes even more difficult. There are so many pitfalls: how you interpret what your partner says, whether you and your partner remain silent and pretend everything's all right when problems come up, how well you listen to each other, how much time you make for real communication, and whether you're able to reveal your true feelings and desires, and then affect an outcome.

Unfortunately, we often don't express ourselves honestly because of our emotional pain and anger, fear of losing control and lashing out at our partner, or worry that our partner might react negatively. Or we are worried about becoming vulnerable. If others know too much about us, they may use the information against us later on.

The feeling that you are not understood, that you can't really talk to your partner, or can't be yourself around him, is one of the first indications of trouble in your relationship. Communication is so complex, yet so important, that we have devoted an entire chapter to it. (Chapter Six, "Communication: What Works and Why.")

Lack of Intimacy. Intimacy, trust, and communication are bound together. Each is dependent on the others. Without trust and honest communication, there can be no intimacy. You have to trust your partner enough to be willing to be vulnerable. When couples are intimate, they are able to reveal their deepest desires, their secret fears, and know that no matter what they say, their partner will continue to love and accept them. Couples who communicate at this level experience their relationship as deeply rich and rewarding. They say they are "soul mates." They are best friends, lovers, and companions, meeting the challenges of life together. They are willing to invest time and energy in each other. You are important to your partner because of who *you* are, not because of your parenting or spousal role, or your career, but because you're *you*.

Just getting back into the relationship with your partner isn't enough. If all the old problems that plagued it before are still there, they will sabotage the new reunion, too. It takes time to discover *what* really went wrong in the relationship and *why*. Although separation is painful, it can be constructive as well, if you take the time to make it so.

Taking Stock of the Situation

This is a good time to examine where you are right now and define your starting point on a plan of action. A good plan depends on knowing where you are now and where you want to go. It's important to know what needs to be changed. The following questions will help you do that. Remember to be honest with yourself.

- Are you newly separated and dealing with raw pain that hurts so much you can barely function? Or have you been separated for long enough that the pain is now tolerable and you have recovered some of your emotional equilibrium?

- How is your health? Have your eating and sleeping habits changed as a result of the separation? Have you let yourself become run-down? Perhaps you've gone the other way and become fanatical about your diet and exercise (trying to look good and win him back)—to the point of overdoing it.

- Do you have children? How are they handling the separation? Have you worked out a custody arrangement with your spouse? Is it working fairly smoothly, or is it causing problems? How has being a single parent affected your relationship with the children?

- Are you having financial problems? If so, what sources of help do you have available, and are you taking advantage of any of them? Have you talked with your partner about sharing responsibility for financial obligations?

- How are you doing at work? Are you able to concentrate, or is your work slipping? Has your career been put on hold while you try to work out this crisis? Have you buried yourself in work to forget the pain, working overtime, taking on too many assignments?

- Do you have a network of family or friends that can provide emotional support or practical assistance? Are you relying on them, or have you become a hermit, wanting just to be left alone?

- How is your social life in general? Do you keep yourself from get-togethers with your married friends, worried that they won't want "a fifth wheel?" Are your friends excluding you, not wanting to choose between you and your spouse, because they have been friends with both of you? Do you dread weekends because there's nothing to do, or are you scheduling activities?

- Do you have religious, spiritual, or philosophical beliefs that you can draw on during this difficult time?

Remember, hope and determination alone are not enough to effect a successful reconciliation. During this time apart, you have a chance to let painful memories fade and begin to uncover the real causes of your problems, and to build a base for a new relationship, starting from where you are now. Doing so now will mean that you must let go—for now—with love.

CHAPTER THREE

How To Detach With Love
and Let Go—for Now

"Are you telling me that I should just stop caring? How is that going to help me get back together with Julie?" Tom was reacting to the suggestion that he should detach himself from the relationship for the time being. Like most people, Tom associated detachment with giving up on the relationship. "I'm very much in love with my wife," he said. "I refuse to even consider the idea."

No one was suggesting to Tom that he give up on loving his wife; quite the contrary. Detachment is not the same as not caring. It is simply stepping aside for a while.

You may feel that because you love your partner, you should be totally immersed in your relationship with him. After all, isn't that what love is all about? As Tom said, "Besides, if I'm not around, she might replace me with someone else. Or, if I stop being involved, maybe I won't feel the same about her."

The intensity of Tom's feelings right now is fueled not only by love, but also by fear. Like Tom, you may be frightened by the idea of being alone and facing the future by yourself, or you may fear that your partner wants to be with someone else. Fear can paralyze you and keep you from turning your attention to the work that lies ahead. When you detach with love, you are lessening the role of fear in controlling your actions. And you are saying to your partner, "I love you and I value you. I release any desire to control you. I'm going to concentrate on me, so that we can grow back together in a stronger way."

Detaching with love involves three steps. The first is to acknowledge that you are in fact powerless over your partner. You
cannot *make* him change his feelings or *make* him love you. You
can control yourself and your own feelings, but not those of
another person, no matter how close you are to him and no matter how much you try.

The second is to recognize that you alone are responsible for
your own well-being and happiness. Just as you cannot *make*
your partner have specific feelings, he cannot *make* you happy or
sad either. You control your own feelings; you decide what emotions you are going to allow.

The third is to focus on yourself. Right now, you are probably
spending most of your time thinking about your partner,
wondering what you can do to bring him back. Your concentra-
tion is on him. Shift your energies to yourself, to the things you
can affect in yourself. Concentrate on your own needs; nurture
and develop your own inner core of being.

Letting Go of Fear

Fear is the basis of the desperate need for attachment. Fear can be
a very disabling emotion. There are many kinds of fear associated
with the ending of a relationship: fear that you'll never get your
partner back, fear that your partner will turn to someone else,
fear of being alone, fear of being on your own, fear of the un-
known . . . the list goes on. These are all possibilities which your
imagination can make excruciatingly vivid. Remember that the
opposite is also a possibility. You could reunite with your partner,
you could make it on your own, and you could increase your self-
confidence by successfully meeting new challenges.

When you experience fear, there is a physical as well as an
emotional reaction. Your stomach knots, your hands get cold and
sweaty, your breathing becomes shallow, your blood pressure
goes up, and your entire body goes into a "fight or flight" state.
Being in this constant state of heightened arousal because of
psychological fear, such as fear of abandonment or fear of loss,
harms you physically and emotionally. You may become worn

down by stress and have difficulty eating, sleeping, or thinking rationally. Because fear can prevent you from achieving the emotional stability you need to start focusing on you, it's important to acknowledge it and then start taking active steps to remedy your situation. Having a plan of action is the best antidote to fear.

Detaching Is a Necessary Step toward Reconciliation

It's normal to have anxiety when confronted with change—like the first day at a new school, a new job, or the first time you were out on your own. If you have a belief system that sustains you, it can be of enormous help. It might be in a Higher Power, it might be in God, or it might be in the belief that all this is happening to you for a purpose and that you will emerge from the experience a stronger person. As you learn that you can manage on your own and be responsible for yourself, your fear will fade. And as it does, you will find it possible to detach with love, and let go—for now.

This is an important step forward to your eventual reconciliation because when you detach with love, you fear less and love more. You take on a new mind-set. Rather than continually saying and thinking, "I need him, I have to be with him," you are able to say, "I care about him and support him. I believe in his ability to make the best decision for himself."

When you detach with love, you acknowledge that you cannot control the other person's emotions and actions but that you trust him to do what is best. No matter what the final outcome is, no matter what decisions the other person makes, you have to trust that he will make the best decision for himself and therefore for the relationship.

> When Tom was finally able to detach and let go, it felt as if a weight had fallen from his shoulders. He told himself, "I love Julie, but I have no control over what she chooses to do. My only control is over myself. I can let Julie know that I love her and trust in her ability to make decisions for herself and that I will be there for her no matter what she chooses to do."

To let someone know that you believe in him this way is the strongest validation of his personhood you will ever make. It takes tremendous courage and faith to tell someone that you love him enough to want whatever will make him happy, that you respect and trust him enough to know he will make the right decision—even if that means he might choose not to come back into the relationship! Paradoxical as it seems, this is a win-win situation for you. Your partner is going to find you much more desirable when you feel confident enough to make such a supportive statement than when you are needy and desperate.

That may be hard for you to accept right now. You may feel a need to get your partner back by demonstrating your love through pursuit and entreaties. Unfortunately, such actions demonstrate only neediness and can turn off your partner. There's something about seeing a person humiliate himself that makes most of us extremely uncomfortable. We want to get as far away as possible.

On the other hand, showing an honest desire for what's best for the other person makes him feel more loved and cherished, and creates a bond of respect for you.

"I Feel So Alone!"

"I dread coming home," Tom confessed. "The apartment feels so lonely and empty without Julie. I just come in and plop down on the sofa and turn on the TV. Don't ask me what I watch; it really doesn't matter. I just keep it on for the sound, for some background noise. There are some guys at work I stop to have a beer with a couple of times a month, but I'm not the type of person who makes friends easily, so I don't have anyone to talk to except my sister. She knows Julie and I have split up, but she's got her own worries. I don't want to keep burdening her with mine."

Like Tom, maybe you're having a rough time right now. You feel lonely, have no one to talk to (or maybe you've talked to all your friends so much they don't want to listen any more), and no strong interests to divert you. If you don't make friends easily or have some outside interests, you may be finding things over-whelming right now. No matter how bad things seem, however, there are things you can do to help yourself in detaching—for now. Here's what you'll want to focus on.

How to Detach and Let Go

The first thing to do is to look for the light at the end of the tunnel. Consciously say to yourself, "Okay, I'm alone now, but that's only temporary. I want to be back with my partner again. I'm going to work on reconciling by focusing on my own growth and the eventual goal of being back with my partner again."

Take Care of Yourself.

Are you eating properly and getting enough sleep? At a time like this, you may be eating poorly and having sleepless nights, con-scious of the empty half of the bed. If you continue this way, your physical condition will weaken, which will make it even harder to get your emotions in balance. Make an effort to maintain your health. Have meals with friends or invite them for dinner. Get some exercise to help you sleep better. Plan activities that get you out of the house. Be good to yourself. You're going to need physi-cal and mental stamina for the work ahead of you.

One of the best things you can do for yourself right now to reduce the stress you are feeling is to exercise. You may want to begin by having your doctor recommend a program that's right for you. Then develop a regular exercise program rather than overdoing exercise when you're stressed out. Make up a schedule and stick to it. You'll feel better, sleep better, and—a great bonus—look better. You'll probably also meet people and make new friends. Perhaps you've always promised yourself that "someday, I'll get into shape, when things have calmed down and I have the time." The time is now.

Relaxation and stress reduction techniques may also be help-ful now. You may doubt that you can relax at a time like this, but remember, relaxation is a skill, and like all skills, it can be ac-quired and practiced. Stress reduction and relaxation techniques come in many variations, but most include deep breathing, muscle relaxation, and visualization to achieve a calming effect. An "Instant Relaxation" technique and a deep muscle relaxation exercise can be found in Appendix B. For additional information, refer to the bibliography for books in this area.

Reach Out To Others

In moments of stress, one of the best things you can do is make contact with others. Call on your family and friends for support. Reach out for warmth and comfort. You need people around you who are willing to listen and help you through this time. Find people who will support you emotionally, who will make you laugh, and get your mind temporarily off your problems.

There is a difference between finding someone who is willing to listen and someone who can help you work things through. Right now you may feel that you want a sympathetic ear more than a counselor. Find someone who will let you express your feelings without judging or giving advice. You might say, "Thank you for just listening and letting me get things off my chest. Later on, I might be ready for suggestions, but right now, I just need empathy—someone to hear me out."

You might be feeling very lonely if you relied on your partner almost exclusively for companionship. But it's never too late to make new friends. What clubs and groups are available in your work setting? How about your church setting? Sign up at a gym or the local YWCA or YMCA. Take the initiative to make friends. There are a lot of people out there who would love to have a new friend just as much as you would.

If you feel you have no one to talk to, or when the time comes that you need more than just a shoulder to cry on or a sympathetic ear, look for a greater level of support through a therapy or support group or individual counseling. Sources of information include your Employee Assistance Program or personnel office at work; your priest, minister, or rabbi; your local Mental Health Association; and the Yellow Pages—look under Pyschologists or Marriage and Family Counselors. Guidelines for choosing an individual therapist are given in Appendix A.

Don't Neglect Your Children And Other Responsibilities

In addition to coping with the stress of separation, you may have children or other family members who rely on you. At this time, when most of your psychic energy is spent dealing with your own pain, it's important to remember those who depend on you. Children need help in dealing with the changes, especially with the loss of someone special to them. Take the time to find out how their day went and to talk about the things that are bothering them. It's vital that you avoid blaming your partner or making your children feel that they're caught in the middle. Reassure them that they are in no way to blame for the separation. Let them know that although the grown-ups are having problems, you both still love them and will continue to take care of them. Because so much else has changed, try to keep their routine as regular as possible. If there are grandparents or other relatives or friends who can help at this time, so much the better. You might call a child psychologist for recommended books on how to help children through separation. Several are listed in the bibliography.

Change Your Environment

Although your focus is on renewing the relationship, the steps you take while doing so will increase your self-confidence and self-esteem. You'll feel that you have grown and changed. Celebrate this growth, the new you, with a symbol that is meaningful to you. You might buy an art print, a new vase, an inspiring record, or new sheets for your bed. You might rearrange the furniture. The key is to recognize that you are growing and changing and to celebrate that change tangibly in your environment.

Focus On You

Begin by taking an inventory of yourself. One of the most meaningful steps you can take at this time, when your self esteem may be at a low ebb, is to discover your strengths. Although you may not think so right now, you have a lot to offer. Now is the time to bolster your own sense of worth. Start a journal. Buy yourself a notebook and every day record your thoughts and feelings. No one else will ever read it, so let yourself be completely honest.

Your journal will be an invaluable record of your growth as you look back and see the progress you've made. On those days when you think nothing you've tried has worked, you can read the journal and see that, in fact, you've come a long way. You'll find that you gain new insights into your situation as you pour out all your emotions. The hardest part is getting started. Here are a few topics and questions which may help you begin taking this inventory of yourself.

Physical Appearance. Describe your general appearance: height, weight, hair color, eye color, figure type, attractive features, things you'd like to improve. Pretend that you're describing yourself to a distant relative whom you've never met.

Personality. Describe your personality. Are you friendly, reserved, shy, frank, open? Do you consider yourself fun-loving, serious, spontaneous, deliberate? Do you communicate freely and easily, or do you guard your speech and choose your words carefully? Do you live for excitement, or do you prefer quiet activities?

Sexuality. How do you view yourself as a sexual being? Do you enjoy sex? Can you communicate your desires, what you like and don't like, honestly? Are you willing to experiment? Have your sexual encounters been satisfying to you and to your partner? Be frank—only you will ever read your journal.

Sociability. Are you happiest in a crowd of people, or do you prefer being with a few close friends? Is it easy for you to make friends, or do you have difficulty approaching others? Are you interested in other people, or do you prefer to be alone?

Mental Habits. Do you collect all the facts meticulously, or do you like to get an overview of a situation, taking it in all at once? Do you investigate every possible solution before taking action, or do you jump in and play a hunch? Do you insist on making decisions yourself, or are you comfortable letting others decide for you? Do you make a decision quickly, or agonize over it for a long time? Once you've made a decision, do you take action immediately, or postpone doing anything until you're sure you're right? Are you creative in your approach, or more traditional, sticking to tried and true methods? Everyone has her own thinking style; it's actually fun trying to look inside your own mind to see how it works.

Career. Are you satisfied with your job, or do you dread going to work? Do you want to continue in your present career or change fields entirely? Does your job challenge you and present opportunities for growth, or does it seem to be a dead end? Do you enjoy the people you work with? Do you see yourself doing the same thing next year, in five years, in ten years? How important is your job to you, compared to your social activities and hobbies? Do you define yourself in terms of your job: "I'm a teacher"?

Family. Do you have children for whom you are responsible? Are they living with you? How is your relationship with them? Do you have family members that rally around and provide support, or are you emotionally (and perhaps physically) distant from your family?

Self-Care. Do you take your good health for granted, never thinking about your physical condition until you're sick? Do you take good care of yourself: eating well, exercising, sleeping enough, getting a physical examination annually? What aspects of your health would you like to improve? Is your home a place where you can relax, nurture yourself, and escape from the stresses of the job?

Spirituality. What are your beliefs, and how strongly do you hold them? Do you have beliefs which sustain you? Are you able to call on a power greater than yourself when the going gets rough? Do your beliefs provide you with strength and solace in times like these?

Schedule Your Activities

In doing this self-assessment, you've taken a good look at yourself. You've thought about who you are, how you are, what you are doing with your life. Like most of us, you probably found some areas you'd like to improve, including taking better care of yourself and lessening stress. Because of the separation, you might have been somewhat self-critical, tending to blame yourself for things you feel you "should" have done. Don't be too hard on yourself at this time. Remember that during the early stages of separation you may not be functioning as well as you were before the breakup. Just bear in mind that this is normal, and that in time you will get back to your usual level of competence. In the meantime, allow yourself more time to complete tasks. Don't don your "Superman" cape and try to overcompensate for your feelings right now. Relax and slow down.

Chances are that you have a lot of things on your mind other than your day-to-day activities. You may find yourself being more forgetful than usual. Just accept that, and leave yourself reminder notes on the refrigerator, in the car, and at work. Double-check your work to be sure you've finished everything. Reassure your friends, family, and supervisor that this absent-mindedness is only a temporary condition and that you'll be back to normal soon. Quite probably, they'll understand and be willing to allow you the time and consideration for not being at your very best during this period.

Be careful, however, that when you relax your schedule that you don't wipe out everything, especially social activities. You need to avoid loneliness now. Keep yourself busy to limit the amount of time available to feel sorry for yourself or to dwell on the negative things that have happened (or are happening) to you. Regain control and avoid loneliness by scheduling your daily activities in detail. Notice where the empty spaces are, and fill them with an activity. It doesn't have to be something strenuous; it can be as simple as a bubble bath, a walk with the dog, or an hour with a good book. The goal is to take back control of your life.

Examine your schedule right now. Does it feature the same routine things: work, driving the children around, chores at home? If you're lonely, it's important to fill your days not just with "make work" but with enjoyable or useful activities. If you have children, it's especially important that you arrange at least a few hours a week of fun just for yourself. If you're alone and time hangs heavy, take a class or weekend seminar, visit the art galleries in your area, or volunteer your time. In fact, volunteering is an excellent way to make you feel better about yourself; it gives you perspective about your plight. When we focus on a problem up close, it sometimes looks and feels more drastic than it really is. Becoming involved with the needs of others can make your problem seem less severe. Your local United Way can point you to a volunteer job in almost any area you are interested in.

Weekends can be especially difficult. Make a point of scheduling your weekends well in advance. Invite someone over for brunch or dinner or to share a movie. If you have a hobby such as painting, pottery, or weaving, take some of your products to a swap meet. You might want to join a special interest group: a hiking or walking club, a folk dance group, a charitable organization. Many newspapers print weekend club activities in the Friday issue; look for something that interests you and gets you out among people.

Counseling

Many people shy away from counseling. Sometimes they feel ashamed of needing help; sometimes they think they should be able to solve their problems themselves. Perhaps you have supportive family and friends and think that, with their help, you can "get through this." But don't expect your family or your best friend to do it all. Although they can listen and be supportive of you, there may come a time when you need some professional counseling care. Perhaps you feel embarrassed at talking about your most intimate problems to friends, or you may not have a support system available at all. Everyone needs someone to talk to. Taking care of youself may mean hiring a therapist to help.

We tend to think that most problems can be solved by the use of common sense. But relationship problems often go beyond the common sense solutions that seemingly would resolve them. That's what makes them so difficult. Consciously you may tell yourself, "I can handle this situation," but inside, a voice may be saying, "I really messed this up. If I had been a better wife, mother, lover . . . he wouldn't have left me." A trained professional can help you deal with old tapes playing in your head that lower your self-esteem.

A therapist can also help you learn how to break with the dysfunctional patterns of communicating and behaving that haven't

worked for you. If you grew up in a troubled household, it's likely that you need to learn new ways of interacting and living with
the people you love—how to communicate, how to create a successful relationship, how to be a good parent—in other crowds,
how to live more functionally. A therapist trained in these areas
can help you acquire these skills.

People often ask *when* to seek the aid of a therapist. If you're
going through a crisis and need help sorting out what's going on
and what your options are, a therapist can provide perspective
and reasssurance, as well as point out factors and consequences
to consider. If you're experiencing several physical symptoms
such as loss of appetite, rapid and severe weight loss, sleep dis-
turbances, difficulty getting out of bed, inability to concentrate,
loss of interest in usual activities, or spontaneous crying spells,
you should seek help immediately. (For information on how to
find a therapist, see Appendix A.)

Track Your Progress
Sometimes, it may seem as if things are never going to get better.
No matter how many times you tell yourself that time will heal
the pain, that things will improve, you may have trouble believing these comforting maxims. This is natural at a time of turmoil.
At first the pain is so intense that it seems as if it will never go
away. The daily crisis seems never ending. But your situation will
change, over time. A good way to measure this change is by keeping track of events and your reactions to them and noting your
improvements. No matter how small your achievements, they
count. You may have heard the Chinese proverb: A journey of a
thousand miles starts with a single step. Your journey toward a
better relationship begins with each thing you do to strengthen
yourself. Your journal is therapeutic in that it allows you to
record your emotions and measure your progress. You've already taken one step by doing your self-assessment. That's your
starting point.

Be sure to acknowledge or reward yourself for the progress
you're making. Every small step moves you forward and increases your confidence. Start a list of "Triumphs" and put it up
on the wall. Every day, note at least one thing that you feel proud

of accomplishing. Perhaps you wanted to call your partner, just to hear his voice, but didn't. You were able to talk with him about the children without bringing up The Other Woman. Maybe you joined a lunchtime walking group, helped your child plan a birthday party, or bought some flowers to brighten your home. Write it down on your "Triumph" list and give yourself a mental pat on the back. Giving yourself positive verbal acknowledgement ("that was good") is very important. Your self-talk to a large extent determines how you feel about yourself and your situation. Go to a movie with a friend, treat yourself to a relaxing massage, do something that allows you to be kind to yourself. The point is that you're always making progress, slowly but surely. By noting where you began, you can see how far you've come.

Few events in life are as painful as separation from the person you love. The questions, "Why? Why did this happen? Where did things go wrong? What could I have done differently? What can I do to bring him back to me?" race around and around in your head. Right now, those questions are natural and inevitable. You can't help thinking about them. You probably just want to mend the rift, get back together as soon as possible, and put all this heartache behind you.

Be patient with yourself. Even though you may not think so now, you will get to a point of feeling better and more hopeful about your life.

CHAPTER FOUR

What Do You Really Want?

You're at a turning point now. Step back and get away from the relationship temporarily to spend time on yourself. Get to know yourself and what you want.

Values are principles that we hold up for ourselves as guideposts for living. They are our most deeply held beliefs. Our values play a prominent role in shaping your goals. Identifying and understanding your most important values gives you a better idea of what you need for your happiness. In Chapter Five we'll show you how to construct a plan for reconciliation, based on your needs and values, and this chapter will serve as a basis for that plan.

Your values are uniquely your own. Some may be general and similar to the ones held by many others—"happiness," "close family", "friends." Others may be specific just to you—such as valuing education, and therefore having a goal such as getting a degree; valuing adventure, and flying off to the South Pacific; or valuing community service and volunteering at a senior citizens' home.

You can also have conflicting values. For example, you may value being part of a twosome, but not want to be accountable to a partner. Perhaps you value honesty and integrity, but sometimes find yourself in situations where those values are compromised (for instance, your manager takes credit for work that you know is someone else's but you don't say anything to bring it out in the open). When too many of your deeply held values are in conflict, as often happens in a troubled relationship, you can begin to feel depressed and anxious because you are compromising your integrity.

How Are Your Values Being Expressed?

Because your values play such an important role in shaping your goals, it's important to know what you really value as opposed to what you think you should value. This is a good time to explore how your values are being expressed in your life. Are you living according to your values, or are they being compromised to the point of making you deeply uncomfortable? How well or poorly are your values being expressed in your relationship? The more you are able to live your life according to the values you hold dear, the more fulfilling and satisfying your life is. The more your values are shared by your partner, the more satisfying your relationship.

Some values may be difficult to express in the relationship as it currently exists. Only when you know what's important to you will you be able to act accordingly.

What Are *Your* Values?

What are your values? What's *really* important to you? The following categories will get you thinking about your own values and what's really important to you. As you read through the questions and answer them, you'll identify those values that you want to incorporate into your life and find out how they fit, or don't fit, into the relationship.

When you mull over these values, ask yourself whether your first response is one that you have been taught to believe is "correct" or whether it reflects your own deeply held beliefs. Think through what living or not living according to that value in your life would mean to you. Perhaps you value independence, while a mutual relationship depends on interdependence. Do you say you want a child because your family believes that children complete a marriage, or because you want to enjoy nurturing and raising children? Do you value job security because you have been taught that it's more important to have a steady income than to take the risks that might be associated with moving from career to career? Do you value an attractive personal appearance, even though you were raised to believe that "beauty is only skin deep?" Do you value having power over others, even though you were taught that cooperation is more important? When your values are in conflict, you have to look for ways to satisfy conflicting needs or decide which values take precedence over others. Remember, there are no "right" answers. There's only what is right for you.

Personal Values

What value do you place on love? Do you consider it more important than personal achievement? How much financial security do you need? How important is a good sense of humor? Loyalty? Friendship? What importance do you place on such values as self-respect, peace of mind, good health, freedom, comfort, achievement, personal growth, status, adventure, stability, excitement, fame? Which could you sacrifice, and under what circumstances?

Relationship Values

Do you need a relationship in which you spend a great deal of time together, or are separations and separate activities all right? Do you have to feel needed in a love relationship? Do you want a mutual relationship? Do you want to be involved in your partner's career or business? Do you want to make decisions jointly, or are you satisfied to let your partner make decisions without consulting with you?

Partner Values

How much do you value communication, trust, intimacy, interdependence? Do you want a partner who will support you in your career and be proud of your achievements, or are you content to be the supportive partner? Are you willing to provide the primary source of income, or do you believe your partner should do so? Do you require absolute fidelity, or would you be willing to "look the other way" under certain circumstances? Do you need to be the most important focus in your partner's life, or are you willing to play a secondary role? Can you accommodate a partner whose sexual needs differ significantly from your own? Do you value spontaneity and a sense of fun in your partner? Security and reliability? How important are appearance, honesty, sincerity, respect, success, loyalty, fidelity, and the ability to commit?

Obviously, it is unlikely that any partner will combine all the qualities you desire. But which are most important to you? There are probably two or three qualities which are absolutely essential. They are the characteristics which probably led you to enter the relationship and kept you there. Unless these values have changed, they are the "musts" in order for the relationship to endure.

Family Values

How do you weigh the needs of your children or partner against your own needs? Do you want active involvement from your partner in child rearing, or are you willing to take on the major tasks? Do you treasure your ties to a close-knit family that gets together frequently, or do you prefer to keep the focus on your own immediate family? Are there family traditions that are important to you, or are you trying to break away from customs that no longer work for you?

Work Values

Is working or having a career important to you? Do you need power and status? Do you want to be recognized for your skills? Are you motivated to achieve outstanding success? Do you seek to be an entrepreneur or to climb to the top of the corporate ladder? Do you think of your work as a job or as a career? Do you work primarily for the income or for the satisfaction? Do you like working with people, or would you prefer to work alone?

Spiritual Values

Do you have a personal belief system or philosophy of life which inspires you and sustains you in all times, or do you feel that you are a victim of chance and luck? Do spiritual or religious beliefs play an important part in your life, or do you ignore or downplay such beliefs?

Setting Your Priorities

The reason to identify your values is so that you can prioritize them. You did this to some extent as you went through the previous questions. For example, when you thought about the values you have for work, you may have mentally assigned a higher priority to the money you make from your job than to the intrinsic satisfaction of the job itself. This is your chance to examine your needs and desires closely and find out what you really want. We all think we want the obvious things—happiness, love, security, good health—but if you watch your actions for contradictions, you might discover that there are things *you* value even more. We want you to be thinking about what's important to you, so that you can *focus* your attention and energies.

Go back through the previous values and identify *two* values in each category that are the most important to you. Please keep in mind that these are your own values and not someone else's. What do you value most? Take your time coming up with these top priorities. Before, when you identified your values, you were thinking about *everything* you value. Now, in order to create a well-focused plan of reconciliation, narrow your list to those two values in each category that are the most important to you. Note: what was important to you as a teenager and as a newlywed might be different right now. In the left-hand column, we have listed one person's choices from each category. List yours in the right-hand column.

<u>**EXAMPLE**</u>	<u>**YOUR VALUES**</u>

PERSONAL VALUES

    1. Marriage/relationship   1. _____

    2. Family   2.

PARTNER VALUES

    1. Fidelity   1. _____

    2. Honesty   2. _____

RELATIONSHIP VALUES

    1. Trust   1. _____

    2. Friendship   2. _____

FAMILY VALUES

    1. Shared Parenting   1. _____

    2. Stable Family   2. _____

WORK VALUES

    1. Satisfaction   1. _____

    2. Recognition   2. _____

SPIRITUAL VALUES

    1. Spirituality   1. _____

    2. Spiritual Growth   2. _____

How Well Does the Relationship Fit Your Values?

Now that you can see what your most important values are, how well does the relationship mesh with them? Does your relationship allow for those needs that are the most important to you? How much do you find yourself compromising and accommodating? Everyone has to make some adjustment between his personal ideals and the demands of a relationship. Much of the time it's possible to shift values without too much inner turmoil. But sometimes there's a big gap between what you value and what's really going on in your life.

When there's a bad fit between your ideals and your actions, anger, depression or guilt can set in. For example, you may value fidelity, but accept explanations that your partner spends time with an old girlfriend purely as "friends," despite strong indications to the contrary. Or, you may value shared child rearing, yet find yourself taking on most of the responsibilities as your husband engages in activities without you. If many ideals in your relationship have been compromised, you may want to face the issue clearly and ask yourself how many of your values you are willing to do without or modify. For example, are you willing to forgo your partner's support or validation of your career, if it means achieving your value of an intact family? What if you value achievement and your husband feels that you should spend less time on your job and more with the family? Are you willing to give up a degree of candor in your communications if it means avoiding accusations and quarrels? Is having an exciting sexual relationship a satisfactory trade-off for not sharing household responsibilities?

Sometimes it's difficult to separate out what you "should" want from what you *do* want. One way to resolve this dilemma and find out what you really value is to watch what you do, as opposed to what you say. For example, you might say, "I value honesty in my relationship," but skirt around certain issues, for fear of what might happen if you confronted them openly. In that case, what you value most is maintaining the relationship, rather than openly confronting issues that might change it—whether to improve or destabilize. Watch what you actually do; actions speak louder than words and can give you insight as to what is most important to you.

If You Need Help Finding Out What You Want

There are times when your emotions are in such a state of turmoil that it's not possible to rationally analyze your needs and motivations. Hidden agendas often need to be uncovered in order to identify your goals and effectively attain them. If you are having difficulty deciding which values are truly the most important to you, look for help in clarifying your thinking either in a support group or through counseling.

Some values you hold are absolute and will brook no compromise. But on many other points, there is flexibility. Your goal is to identify those values on which you are flexible and those values on which you have to stand firm for the sake of your own mental health and happiness. There is no such thing as a "perfect" relationship, but you do want one in which most of your basic needs for happiness can be met. In the next chapter, we'll help you translate your values into a specific plan for reconciliation.

CHAPTER FIVE

Creating Your Plan Of Action

"When a friend told me I should have a plan for getting Lynn back, I thought that sounded so manipulative," said John. "But the more I thought about it, the more it made sense. It was becoming clear that she wasn't going to come back just because I kept telling her how much I loved and needed her. In fact, it seemed to drive her away, because I sounded so desperate. The more emotional I became, the more distant she was. I realized I needed a plan, something that would help me put emotions aside for the moment and focus more constructively on working toward reconciliation. I had to have a plan of action if I was going to do the things that would lead to reconciliation with Lynn."

Does this sound familiar? Did you notice that, as you told your partner how much you love her and how much you want her back, your pleas were falling on deaf ears? It's unlikely that your partner will be swayed by protestations of undying love or promises that you'll try harder to make her happy. She may have made some gestures out of kindness or pity that encouraged you temporarily, but you're in this for the long run. And over time, displays of neediness will only convince your partner that she was justified in leaving you. Feeling powerless makes you feel that you aren't in control of your life, thus lowering your self-esteem. It's a vicious circle.

Creating a plan for reconciliation begins by setting goals that derive from your own values. The you can assess how your values fit into the relationship. First you'll need to regain your power.

Regaining Your Power

When you want your partner back, how can you stop acting needy and desperate? The key is to stop focusing on your partner and start focusing on yourself. Dwelling on the separation won't bring your partner back. You need a concrete plan of action that will help you focus on the work to be done to make reunion possible. You need to set some goals. When you have goals of importance to you, you become much more active and purposeful. At this point, it's important to summon up these positive feelings, and work toward fulfilling your goals in order to create your new relationship.

If you're feeling hurt, confused, angry and lonely, you may not be certain that you have the ability to create a plan right now. That's understandable; your self-confidence has taken a blow. This loss of confidence is another reason why it's important that you be organized and focused on your objectives. Remember that your ultimate goal is not just reconciliation, but reunion into a lasting relationship that is stronger, healthier, and more loving than it was before.

You have to know what you want before you can plan to get it. By identifying your values and assigning priorities to them, you've taken the first step toward setting the goals that help you get what you want. You're getting back in charge of your life. Instead of reacting to events, you're becoming proactive—determining what you want to bring about for your future.

The goals you set will become your plan of action for working toward reconciliation. They will incorporate your values, so that you can live out what's important to you. For example, if you value intimacy, one goal is to be able to communicate effectively in order to achieve it. A goal is the bridge that takes you from a mere wish ("I wish I had her back") to actions that help you achieve the wish ("I'm going to work toward being able to talk with my partner without voicing recriminations").

Setting Goals

Without a plan, you have little control over what happens. It could be something wonderful and worthwhile, but then again, it could be a catastrophe. Planning is critical at this stage of separation because it enables you to build the bridge to reconciliation. A goal lets you plan for the bigger picture by setting tangible tasks that can spell the difference between wishful thinking and bringing about a desired outcome. Right now, you may be feeling unsure and vulnerable, not knowing what to do next. You may think that your partner holds the key to what will happen. You may feel that you have very little control over what happens in your relationship; after all, he's the one who decides whether he'll come back to you or not. It's true that your partner will make that decision, but that's his control over his life. You are the one who can control your life. With a plan of action, you regain control of your life. You have something solid to hold onto when events are spinning all around you. Here are some principles to keep in mind as you start setting your goals.

Find Your Balance
When you think about goals right now, you probably have one primary goal: to get back together with your partner. While that's the central goal, it should not be your only one. As we said earlier, at this point, reunion should not even be your primary goal. Your number one goal right now should be taking care of yourself. This involves a variety of areas, such as the physical (eating and sleeping better, exercising regularly), intellectual (taking a class in something that interests you), and emotional (making and sustaining friendships). Keep your goal of reconciliation in sight, but don't let it crowd out everything else.

Set Goals That Are Important to YOU
It's important that your goals be what you truly want rather than what is socially approved. For example, don't enroll in a night class just because your family says you should. Make your goals personal and meaningful to you, so that you will be motivated to work toward them.

Set Small, Achievable Goals

Believing in yourself may be the most difficult part of goal-setting for you right now. Make your goals achievable. For example, rather than setting a goal like "having dinner with Michael this weekend" when Michael hasn't spoken to you in two months and doesn't return calls, a more achievable goal would be "have Michael taking my calls within six weeks." The key is to strike a balance between a goal that is too easy and one that is overwhelmingly difficult.

Take it One Step at a Time

You need signposts along the way to let you know you're on the right track. Even though your ultimate goal is reconciliation, take it one step at a time. This month, work on getting back your mental and physical equilibrium. Next month, initiate contact with your partner with a note or on the telephone. The month after that, the two of you might meet in a nonthreatening situation (not a date) to share what you're doing. Slowly but surely, as you meet each goal, you'll gain confidence. You will be able to see that you are making progress toward your ultimate desire.

Put Your Goals in Writing

Until they are written out, your goals will be fuzzy. When you write concrete goals down, you make them clear and definite in your mind so that they become more than wishful thinking. For example, "I want Michael to take me to the company picnic next month, so that Carol will see that we're together again" focuses "someday" and "one of his old girlfriends" into specific terms. It's much easier to achieve a goal when you have a blueprint that shows you how. Written goals serve as tangible, confidence-inspiring targets that you can see come to life.

Make a Timetable

Create a timetable that focuses on you as much as on the relationship. In addition to setting target dates involving your partner, also include dates for your own achievements: joining an exercise class, starting a course, finishing a self-help book. In scheduling targets involving your partner, be prepared to be flexible. Rather than writing down, "Win Michael back by June 1," you can write "Communicate honestly by spring." Having a timetable keeps you on track so that you can follow your plan's progress. Checking off your achievements motivates you to keep working even when things seem to be slowing down. Remember, it takes persistence and determination to achieve your goal.

Creating Goals that Reflect Your Values

With that in mind, it's time to turn each of the values you identified in Chapter 4 into goals. An example is provided to get you started.

ONE PERSON'S VALUES AND GOALS

PERSONAL VALUES	PERSONAL GOALS
1. Marriage/relationship	1. To be part of a loving couple.
2. Family	2. To provide a good home for my children.

PARTNER VALUES	PARTNER GOALS
1. Fidelity	1. Absolute fidelity from my partner, and the peace of mind that comes from knowing that he wants to be faithful.
2. Honesty	2. We can trust each other totally.

RELATIONSHIP VALUES	RELATIONSHIP GOALS
1. Trust	1. I want absolute trust in my relationship.

2. Friendship

2. My partner is my best friend.

FAMILY VALUES

1. Shared Parenting

2. Stable Family

FAMILY GOALS

1. Child rearing a joint activity, with my partner sharing the responsibility. (I don't want to be a "single parent" in my marriage.)

2. Family the most stable and secure thing in our lives. Children feeling safe and loved.

WORK VALUES

1. Satisfaction

2. Recognition

WORK GOALS

1. Helping people through work.

2. Recognition for being productive.

SPIRITUAL VALUES

1. Belief in a Higher Power

2. Spiritual Growth

SPIRITUAL GOALS

1. Feeling secure in the knowledge that the Lord is watching over me.

2. Continued growth in knowledge and awareness, searching for greater understanding.

Identifying The Obstacles

You have already taken one of the most essential steps in planning for your reunion, and that is to identify what's most important to you so that you can decide how to achieve it. The next step is to find out what might stand in your way. Here are some typical obstacles you may encounter:

Negative Self-talk

In order to succeed, you must believe that you *can* and counter your negative thoughts with positive self-talk. "He'll never come back," is self-sabotaging talk. Repairing your relationship may not be easy, and it's not always possible to turn a dysfunctional relationship into a mutually satisfying one, but you *must* begin by being positive.

Fear of the Commitment

Now that you've identified your goals, the next step is to make a commitment to yourself to reach them. This is your promise to yourself that you are going to do whatever it takes to turn a desire into a reality. Your plan reflects your values and goals; it includes the things most important to you. Commitment is the fuel that focuses you. Make the commitment and keep believing that you can succeed.

Impatience

Patience is essential. Be willing to invest the time it will take to achieve it. A desire to either "have it all now or just get it over with and end it," may lead you to think about just walking away from the situation without giving yourself a chance to evaluate it carefully. Take this opportunity to focus on *you*, before you make any rash decisions.

Fear of Being Ridiculed for Your Decision

"What if others think I'm foolish to want my partner back?" We all have a fear of rejection or ridicule. Suppose you do want to reunite with someone who was unfaithful to you. You tell your best friend of your goal, and she immediately tries to talk you out of the plan. She might be doing so from the kindest of motives, sincerely thinking that you are making a mistake. The solution to this obstacle is very simple: Keep your goals to yourself unless you're sure of your friend's support. It's important to keep a positive attitude.

Fear Of Failure

It's natural to be afraid that you won't succeed. What if you put in all this effort, turn a deaf ear to those who think your plan is foolish, follow through on all the steps, and still don't succeed? First of all, if you follow through on everything that needs to be done, you will have the satisfaction of knowing that you have done everything possible. You will never blame yourself with "What if I had done this or that?" Second, by going through all these steps, you will have made an enormous investment in yourself that will pay off in every area of your life and give you increased self-respect and confidence. Third, you will be able to enter any new relationship with the self-esteem and skills that give it the best chance for success.

Visualizing the Benefits of Achieving Your Goal

Think about the positive things that are going to happen when you accomplish your goal. Take a few moments and daydream about the good things to come. They can be silly and small ("I can't wait to give Michael that red bikini underwear I bought him for Valentine's Day right before we broke up!") or important ("Our daughter will be overjoyed when we're a whole family again"). Create an image of you and your partner together again. Make it as detailed and vivid as possible. By focusing on the desired end result, you allow your subconscious mind to work with you in bringing it about. There are a number of excellent books on how to do visualizations. You may want to read up on the positive ways to empower your ideals.

CHAPTER SIX

Communication: What Works And Why

Communication is the essence of a relationship—it's how we connect with others and express our thoughts, feelings, hopes, fears, and dreams. Everything we do is a form of communication—our facial expression, our body stance, our tone of voice, and all the other ways that we present ourselves and interact with others. When we communicate, we share ourselves, hoping that we'll be listened to, accepted, and understood. When we're not, we feel that something important is missing. We say that "communication has broken down."

No one has to tell you how important communication is to a relationship. Of all the factors that make for a successful relationship, communication, along with commitment, is the most vital. In good marriages, communication is the tie that binds couples strongly together. In relationships that need mending, lack of communication is one of the first signs of trouble. One of the primary problems you are no doubt facing right now is how to open the lines of communication in order to mend and build your relationship.

Have You Lost Your "Soulmate"?

Have you experienced those rare moments when you felt totally "in tune" with your partner, when you both seemed to be "on the same wavelength?" We treasure the times when, despite all the differences, we experience the same feelings in the same way. At those moments, we feel total oneness, understanding, and acceptance. It's what people mean when they refer to their partner as their "soulmate."

> Larry described it best when he talked about his marriage to Marge. "So many times," he said, "we don't even have to say a word. It's like I know what she's thinking, or she knows what I'm thinking, and we'll both say the same thing at the same time. Here's a good example. The other night we were watching a movie, but my mind kept going back to my ill father. Suddenly, Marge turned to me and said, 'I think you should fly back to New York and see your father.' That kind of thing happens to us all the time."

Larry and Marge have an ability to empathize and communicate with each other at a deep level. How can *you* overcome the separateness that divides you and your partner? Why is it so hard to communicate? Let's take a look at some of the main obstacles.

Why Communication Is So Difficult

When your relationship is in trouble, you most want and need to reach an understanding. So why is it that, even with the best intentions, it's so easy to misunderstand or be misunderstood?

Have you ever tripped over your own words and said, "Oh, that came out all wrong. What I *really* meant to say was ... " Perhaps you think you heard one thing and your partner really said another. Haven't you ever shown up for an appointment and found out that you misunderstood the time or the day that it was scheduled? Most people have had that experience.

Or maybe you find yourself disagreeing on the meanings of words. A friend says, "What a beautiful red," and you answer, "That's not red, that's rose." Or, your partner says, "That house is too small," and you answer, "I think it has plenty of room." Big, small, good, bad, hot, cold, all mean different things to different people.

But, since we're all unique individuals, with our own unique backgrounds, expectations, and beliefs, we all experience events differently. You might believe that if you communicate well, your partner will agree with what you're saying. But communication is more than reaching agreement. Empathic listening means that we allow our partner to express himself and try to understand his point of view. We accept this view as valid for *him*, even though we may not agree with it. In other words, knowing how to listen is just as important as knowing how to talk.

How to Talk So Your Partner Will Listen and Listen So Your Partner Will Talk

Studies have shown that there are key factors that govern how we experience our environment and perceive others. One of these factors is our individual style of processing information, which literally determines how we experience the world around us. There are three basic modes of perception: visual, auditory, and kinesthetic. Most people are visual—they "see" what you mean—and *how* they see things governs how they feel about them. Others are auditory—things "sound good" to them, or else they "don't like the sound of that." The third group are kinesthetic—they "have a feel for things" or they go by their "gut reactions."

Misunderstandings are most likely to occur when two people have different predominant modes of processing information—for example, when a person who is predominantly auditory gives verbal instructions to a person who is predominantly visual.

"Do You See What I Mean?"
Visual people tend to forget very quickly what has been said. Out of sight is literally out of mind—words seem to disappear into thin air. So if you're exasperated with your partner because you keep asking him to do something and he hasn't, or he never remembers to stop and bring home what you called about, try writing notes and leaving them where he'll be sure to see them—like the dashboard of the car or the door you want him to fix.

"Tell Me That You Love Me."

Auditory people love to talk, they describe things in great detail. They think in words, rather than images or feelings. They like to keep in frequent verbal contact, and they *will* remember what you said. To get your point across, talk to your verbal partner or make a tape for him.

"I Know How You Feel."

A kinesthetic person would rather hold your hand and commune silently than explain verbally how much you mean to him. It's not that he doesn't care—it's that words don't mean as much to him as the reassuring pressure of a hand. He's more apt to wash your car as a way of communicating that he cares. But if you're verbal you might want to hear the words, "I love you." For the kinesthetic person, actions speak louder than words. Hold the kinesthetic person's hand, or hug him as you tell him that you need to hear, "I love you." This way, he'll *feel* what you mean.

One of the most important things you can do to improve communication between you and your partner is to become aware of your own processing and communication style. Are you predominantly visual, auditory, or kinesthetic? The following check list will help you determine *your* processing and communication style. Check the column that is true for you.

WHAT IS *YOUR* COMMUNICATION STYLE?

	YES	NO
I need to *see* things to understand them	_____	_____
I like to get the big *picture*	_____	_____
I want people to *see* my point of view	_____	_____
For me, *seeing* is believing	_____	_____
Appearance is important to me	_____	_____
I remember *conversations*	_____	_____
I can *talk* and work at the same time	_____	_____
I don't have to look at some-one to *talk* to him	_____	_____
I often *talk* to myself when I'm deciding something	_____	_____
I like to *tell* all the details when I *talk* about something	_____	_____
My *feelings* are easily hurt	_____	_____
I go by my gut *feelings*	_____	_____
It's easier for me to learn by *doing*	_____	_____

I *use my hands*
when I talk   _____   _____

I can *commune*
with someone I'm
close to without
talking   _____   _____

If you answered "yes" to the first five statements, you're primarily visual, and you perceive the world in a visual way. You would rather see a picture than hear something described. The saying, "One picture is worth a thousand words," describes you. You're likely to want people to look at you while you're talking to them in order to feel that they're paying attention. It's probably easier for you to find your way to a strange place with a map, than by listening to directions. And if you don't have your shopping list you might wonder, "Now what did I come to here to buy?"

The next five statements are for auditory people. If you're auditory you remember everything word for word, you can sit in a meeting or a class and never take notes. You can tell your partner in detail what he said, or remember detailed instructions. You can converse with your partner even if you're in another room. You carry on a lot of inner conversations. You're usually comfortable talking in front of large groups and can "think on your feet" and field questions easily.

The last five statements describe people who are kinesthetic. Do you become tearful in sad movies, use your hands when you talk, find your stomach tightening when someone else is tense, and learn better by actually doing? If you have these traits, you are kinesthetic. Things "feel" either right or wrong to you. When things don't "feel" right it disturbs you. You go with your "hunches" or "gut reactions." You relate easily to other people's feelings and, especially, want your partner to be aware of yours. You empathize readily—you can actually *feel* the other person's happiness or pain.

Most people have one dominant mode of accessing and processing information and one or two secondary modes. Some people can use all three modes equally well. Because they use all modes easily, they're usually excellent communicators. They can always "talk the other person's language," whatever mode that might be.

Difficulties arise when partners start talking right past each other, because they're not communicating in the language mode that the other prefers. Probably one of the most common arguments that arise between visual and auditory partners stems from the request, "Look at me when I'm talking to you." The auditory person answers, "I can hear you" (while reading the newspaper, or watching TV, or even from another room!). What he doesn't realize is that a visual person *needs* her partner to look at her while she talks. She has to be able to *see* that he is paying attention and understands what she's saying. She needs to look at him in order to "see" his reactions to what she is saying. Otherwise she feels that her partner just doesn't care, or hasn't heard.

To find out your partner's primary communication mode, go back to the "What Is Your Communication Style" checklist that you filled out for yourself, and this time, ask your partner to fill it out. Then, when you are talking with him, observe how he uses his predominant communication style. The next time you want to communicate something important, be sure to put it in his processing mode so that your message has maximum impact. For example, if you want to build more intimacy with your partner you could say:

> VISUAL: "I really enjoy *seeing* us do things together. It seems like we've become much closer."

> AUDITORY: "When I *listen* to you *talk* about our future, I can *hear* how much closer we've become."

> KINESTHETIC: "It *feels good*, like we're really *close* when we spend time together."

As you become more skilled at talking in your partner's preferred mode, you'll notice that communication improves. Keep in mind that unless you literally speak his language he won't fully see, hear, or feel what you're trying to convey. Ideally, each of you will care enough to learn about the other's preferred style and when you do, you'll have a better chance of really "tuning in" to each other.

Principles of Effective Communication

In addition to speaking to your partner in his preferred mode, there are a number of basic principles of good communication that have been time-tested and found effective. If you familiarize yourself with them and practice using them until they become second nature, you'll find that communication between you and your partner improves.

Practice these communication skills regularly. At the beginning they may seem awkward and artificial, but give them a chance and use them; eventually they'll come naturally. Maybe you'll need to modify some of these techniques so they fit your own personal style and feel more natural. That's OK. *Whatever you do, keep practicing!* Remember, your goal is to reunite with your partner and to make your new relationship better than ever. One of the most important ways you'll do that is by communicating effectively.

At this point, you may be separated with very little or only hostile exchanges with your partner, you may be communicating regularly but still experiencing difficulties and frustrations in getting your point of view across, or you may be at the point where you're actively discussing reconciliation. You may even have already reconciled and be looking for a way to make sure things work out this time. Whatever point you're at, communication is the vital key to success. So even if you're apart and not currently having a lot of contact with your partner, read these examples and see how you can apply them—either now, or in the future. Because when you do get back together, being able to use them will be essential to your successful reunion.

1. *Tell how you feel.* Use "I" statements, such as: "I want, I feel . . ." to let your partner know what the impact of his behavior is on you.

EXAMPLE: "Even though we're separated, I want us to remain friends. When you make decisions about the children without consulting me, I feel that my desires are unimportant." Or, when you move toward reconciliation: "When we talk honestly to each other, I feel really close to you. I want us to continue sharing our thoughts and feelings with each other."

You can't change your partner's wants or feelings, but you can clearly express your own *without blaming*. That's a real key. Wanting and feeling are automatic—you can't change them by an act of will. You also can't expect your partner to change because you feel a certain way, but you *can communicate* your feelings clearly. No matter how long you've been together, your partner may not know how you feel about a situation. When you clearly state how you feel and what you want *without blaming*, you give him the opportunity to respond without feeling defensive.

2. *Ask for what you want.* Ask for what you want directly. Directness goes with "I" statements. Instead of saying "You never call when you say you will" or "Why don't *you* ever take the children for an outing?" both of which assign blame, state your wants directly.

EXAMPLE: "I'd like us to start building trust. If you want to join us for a picnic on Sunday, we'll be leaving here at 11:00."

3. *Be brief.* Be brief when you talk to avoid overloading your partner and having him tune out. An excellent exercise is to state your wants in 25 words or less.

EXAMPLE: "I need your help on Saturday to take Bruce to Little League while I take Joni to the dentist."

Communicating like this not only shows respect but gets better results than saying, "I'm fed up with your being so irresponsible; why don't you ever think of us instead of just doing what's convenient for you?" By omitting blame, you reduce your partner's natural reaction to defend himself, and you create an opportunity for change.

4. *Be specific.* Be specific instead of using vague words like "close-ness" and "caring." Rather than saying something like, "You never show me you care," which is a blaming statement that really doesn't let your partner know what you want, translate your desires into specific behaviors that you would like at certain times. This is especially important as you begin to move toward reconciliation.

> EXAMPLE: "When we get together again, I'd like us to develop more closeness by sitting down together for 15 minutes when we get home from work and sharing what went on during the day."

This may seem somewhat artificial at first, but your partner may have often felt really confused by demands for "more considera-tion," "more caring," or "more intimacy," if he's not sure of what you mean by these requests. Even though it may seem difficult at first, asking for what you want directly is a communication skill that both of you can learn to use effectively.

5. *Watch what your body language is saying.* Be aware of your body language. If your words say one thing, but your body posture and voice tone say something else, you're sending a mixed mes-sage. Your partner will feel either confused or resentful. He may decide that you really don't know what you want or will choose to respond to the message that's most convenient.

For example, perhaps you have trouble expressing anger and therefore tend to cover up your feelings. At the same time that you try to express anger about a situation you may smile ner-vously and speak in a soft voice so that you're not taken seriously.

If you feel discomfort when expressing yourself about a situation that you feel strongly about, rehearse first in front of a mirror. Practice taking a deep breath and using your whole body when you speak, so that your tone is deeper and more assertive. Make sure that your body stance and facial expression fits in with the message you want to convey.

EXAMPLE: You stand comfortably straight, with feet apart, look directly at your partner and say in a firm voice tone, "I feel disappointed and angry when you cancel our plans at the last minute. It makes me feel that you don't respect my time. I realize emergencies can come up, but I want you to keep your committ-ments with me."

6. *Present alternatives.* Give your partner some alternatives. We're all more likely to respond positively to situations when we have some control over outcomes. Providing options helps set the stage for mutual problem-solving.

EXAMPLE: "There's a good movie playing. Let's get a baby sitter and go see it Saturday night. But if your brother comes over, we could go Sunday instead."

7. *Use active listening.* Let your partner know she has your full at-tention. Maintain eye contact, and nod, or give verbal cues that show understanding or agreement. It also helps to restate in your own words what your partner has said to make sure you under-stand.

EXAMPLE: "It sounds like you really want to get out and do something. Tell you what—if Andy comes over Saturday night, we'll go see the movie on Sunday for sure."

8. *Show empathy.* Give your partner feedback in a way that shows you understand his position, even if you don't agree with it. Let him know your reaction in a way that doesn't require either of you to justify yourselves but leaves the door open for negotiation and change.

EXAMPLE: "I understand that it's important for your career to put in a lot of overtime, but I feel lonely and I miss you when you're not here."

What to Do If Your Partner Doesn't Want to Communcate

Despite your good communication skills, your partner may simply not want to talk to you. He cuts you off, leaves the room, changes the topic, or in some other way makes clear that whatever you wanted to discuss is a subject that he would prefer to ignore. Or, since you have separated, perhaps he won't return your calls, or is hostile when you do talk. This can be very frustrating. While you want to put all your cards on the table, solve problems, and come to a resolution, your partner may insist that there is no problem, or that it's already been solved, or that he's tired of talking about it. In spite of your best efforts, it appears that the in-depth verbal processing you want so badly is not going to take place. What should you do?

Trying to get a resistant partner to open up and start talking about issues of concern to you can be a frustrating goal which often makes problems worse. If the issue has been previously addressed, step back and identify just what emotional need you want fulfilled by your partner. Is it acknowledgment? Is it reassurance? Is it comfort? If the issue is emotionally laden, the tendency is to want to pursue it. However, rather than focus on the specific topic, express your underlying feelings. Go back to Step One and use "I" statements in a nonthreatening, nonblaming manner, letting your partner know clearly what you need.

> EXAMPLE: Instead of saying something like, "Are you sure you don't want to see Gloria any more?," say something like, "Despite the fact that everything has been great since we've been back together, I still keep getting flashes of you together with Gloria. It makes me feel very anxious—I need to hear you say that I'm the only one in your life."

There may be other times when you want to explore issues that your partner clearly is uncomfortable with. If your partner avoids discussion, you may become angry and doubt that he's really committed to the relationship. "Why doesn't he want to work this out?" you ask. There are a number of reasons that he may be avoiding communication. Here are some common reasons and what you can do about them.

The Issue Has Already Been Dealt With

This may be an issue that has been talked out with your partner and resolved but that continues to haunt you. Your need to reopen it may really be a need for reassurance. When Rita and Paul reconciled, Paul broke off with the girlfriend he had been seeing during the separation. He told Rita that he wanted to be married to her more than anything else in the world. All his actions bore out his commitment to their relationship.

But Rita was unsure. Was Paul still harboring romantic feelings about his former girlfriend? Did he think she was more attractive or sexier than Rita? Rita wanted to know. Specifically, she wanted to hear Paul say that he was sorry about what he had done, that he was crazy to have been with someone else when Rita was still the love of his life, and that no one would ever be able to distract him again.

What You Can Do: It would have been better, when Rita became aware of her need for reassurance, if she had asked for it directly. She could have told Paul, "I love you and trust you but I need reassurance. I need to hear that *I'm* the person who's most desirable to you."

The Issue Feels Too Painful to Discuss

Your partner may be feeling shame or guilt about past actions. Such feelings are very painful, and he may be trying to deal with them by denying them. It can be easier to say "It never happened" about a situation he now regrets than to talk about it and try to explain *why* it happened. As a general rule, the more guilt your partner feels, the more likely he is to deny the situation, try to minimize it, or just refuse to discuss it.

What You Can Do: Recognize that the most important thing is for your partner to confront these painful feelings. Rather than focus on the details of the event, help him to express his feelings about it. "I know it must be very painful for you when you think about how your seeing Gloria affected the level of trust in our marriage. I just want you to know I realize how hard it is to talk about, and I'm willing to just listen any time you're ready."

Your Partner Has a Need for Privacy

Persistent questioning can feel intrusive. Although communication is the heart of a good relationship, demands to "tell me what you're thinking" can feel like an invasion of privacy. Your partner may need to keep a certain amount of information about his activities (however trivial they may be) to himself. This is not out of a desire to keep secrets, but rather a need to feel that certain areas of his life belong to him alone.

What You Can Do: Remind yourself that your partner may need more psychological space than you do. Tell yourself, "It's not really important; if it were, he'd tell me. Right now, he needs it to be *his* secret." We all harbor some thoughts that we do not wish to disclose to our partner.

Your Communication Styles Differ

There are processing and communication styles that don't lend themselves to a great deal of verbal self-examination. For some individuals (especially kinesthetic and visual ones), "putting something away" is literally that. They have filed the matter away permanently and are able to retrieve it only by resurrecting the original painful (or shameful) events in their consciousness and re-experiencing them. Naturally, they are reluctant to do so. One year after Tom and Paula's reconciliation, Tom has still not divulged certain activities of his during their separation. He insists that "It's over. It belongs in the past."

What You Can Do: If this is your situation, it helps to remind yourself that there are some things you may never know, but that your partner loves you, and the things you don't know are probably irrelevant to your *new* relationship. Seek your assurance from his actions.

Speaking from Your Heart

Although you've acquired proven tools for communicating more effectively, you may still have questions about how to deal with specific issues and circumstances. Many of them will be answered in other chapters. The guiding principle to remember is this: the most important tool is you—*you* are the message. The more honestly and openly you speak, the more simply and clearly you reveal what is in your heart, the more likely it is that you will open deeper channels of communication.

When you speak from the heart there is no pretense, no blaming, no covering up. You are simply stating what is true for you. Because you are speaking from your truth, without requiring any response from your partner, you are establishing communication at the deepest level. It is very likely that you will trigger an equally honest response in your partner. Even if he is not able to respond equally openly at this time, you will have established a bridge that will grow stronger as you continue to speak from your heart. This is what empathy is about. Empathy is your communication bridge.

CHAPTER SEVEN

Are You Ready To Reconcile?

Throughout this book, we have placed the emphasis on *you*. Our goal in these chapters has been to encourage you to evaluate your life, look inward, and decide what is working and what isn't. When you know yourself well enough to determine what you need and want, you have a better chance of reconciling into a relationship that will last.

In previous chapters, we talked about how to regain control of your life and work toward reconciliation through such steps as identifying your values and then setting goals aimed at achieving them. Although you love your partner and want to be together again, you've accepted responsibility for your own life. You've examined your ability to communicate on a more intimate level and developed a plan for focusing your emotions into constructive actions. In other words, you're loving your way back into the relationship.

Don't Rush It!

You may have decided that if the relationship is to work for you, some basic changes will have to be made. Be sure that before you consider reunion, you've created the foundation for the type of relationship you want. Don't let your need for love and security rush you into a situation for which you are not emotionally prepared. If you're still waking up in the middle of the night feeling anxious and hurt, it might be tempting to get back together just to ease that pain and loneliness. Work through your pain, and don't consider getting back together until you are feeling emotionally strong and healthy. The times when you don't feel strong, and you long for your partner, may lead you to consider a premature reunion. If you find yourself lapsing to a previous stage, go back and reread the chapter in this book that applies. Be sure that you are ready to move forward. For example, unexpressed, pent up anger may cause you to lash out violently at your partner and destroy your chances for a successful reconciliation. This does not mean that you should repress your feelings, but rather that you need to express them in a way that does not undermine the relationship.

Whether you're working toward reconciliation alone, or whether your partner shares the same goal, you'll want to evaluate your readiness to be back in the relationship. Have confidence. *You* possess many of the resources needed to mend your relationship. Looking inward helps you deal with a crisis in a way that increases the possibility of a successful reconciliation. Rather than becoming immobilized by loneliness, or giving up on your relationship, you can see it as an opportunity to rethink what you really want and need in *your* life. As you find your own center of strength, you'll be in a better position to reunite successfully.

Dangers of a Premature Reunion

After all the hard work you've done getting to this point, be careful that you don't rush back prematurely. Being ready to love your way back into the relationship includes being willing to take things slowly. This is difficult to do when every fiber of your being is looking for love, when you lie awake at night just wanting to be held by your partner. Yet that voice in the back of your head might be telling you to wait. How do you decide when the time is right? Is there a best time to get back together with your partner? What will work for *you*? Here are some guideposts to help you make a more logical, well-reasoned decision.

Are the Old Issues Resolved?

You have taken a long look at how you handled yourself during the separation. Now it's time to determine what problems created the separation in the first place. Up to this point, the main focus of concern was your own emotional well-being. As you worked on yourself, some of the roots of your problems may have become apparent. Now, you are more empowered, and you are ready to examine them.

Begin this analysis by listing the symptoms and probable causes (if you can identify them) of the problems leading to the break up of your relationship. A symptom is the specific behavior that disturbs you. The causes are the events or conditions that fostered the symptom(s). For example, "He never introduced me by name to his friends, only as 'the wife,' because thats how his father always introduces his mother" or "He refused to accept any responsibility for childrearing, thinking that was my job since he worked outside the home and I didn't, because he grew up in a home where sex roles were rigidly segregated." For each symptom, write down what you perceive as the cause and what changes need to be made.

Example:
Symptom: He never introduced me by name to his friends, only as 'the wife.'
Cause: That's how his father introduces his mother.
Changes I Would Like: He would learn to introduce me as "My wife, Jane."

Example:
Symptom: He refused to accept any responsibility for childrearing, thinking that was my job since he worked outside the home and I didn't.
Cause: He was brought up to believe in rigid sex roles.
Changes I Would Like: He would agree to share childrearing.

Dividing your list into symptoms, their causes, and the changes that need to be made will give you a good insight as to what needs to be done in the relationship and whether you can expect those symptoms to be resolved. Remember, symptoms are just outgrowths of causes, and in order for the relationship to improve, you need to understand the underlying causes, as well as know *what* changes in behavior you need.

Look at your list carefully. Have the problems been resolved? Some you might have solved yourself, just by becoming more capable. For example, if you had financial problems and you have since gotten a job, that's one problem that might seem less urgent now. If your spouse had a drinking problem, but has been sober for six months and is regularly attending AA meetings, you might feel more confident about the relationship. Some of the problems may have resolved themselves, at least for the time being, without any help. Perhaps your child went off to college, cooling down the arguments you used to have over curfews and car use. Maybe the promotion you were working toward—initiating a furious battle over how much time you already give to your career rather than to your family—went to someone else.

Your partner might have solved some problems on his own, too. He might have decided that your relationship was more important than seeing his old girlfriend. Maybe he changed to a less stressful job and is therefore less irritable, or he is learning to open up and communicate. If the problems seem to have been mostly resolved, that's wonderful, but be cautious. Make sure your new foundation is solid. Remember, insist on the patterns of behavior that work *for* the relationship.

Have *You* Learned New Patterns of Behavior?

Despite Penny's yearning for a closeknit family life, Josh spent most weekends golfing with friends and one or two nights a week out at his favorite club, often not coming home till 1:00 or 2:00 a.m. Before their twins were born, Penny had been able to accompany him, but with two toddlers, it was much more difficult, and Josh made it clear he did not enjoy the company of babies.

Penny loved Josh and remembered their good times with longing, but she was also a devoted mother. It hurt her that Josh was so uninterested in being a parent. She worried about the eventual effect of a distant father on her sons and shared her concerns with Josh. He declared that he felt a need to come and go as he pleased. "I warned you before the boys came," he would tell her.

> "There was a time when I would have screamed at Josh when he came home, or nagged him about his responsibilities to the boys. Now I realize that the more I nagged, the worse things got. Since we separated, Josh has realized how much his home really does mean to him. He and I have been talking about how we could be more of a family. I know he really has trouble relating and playing with the children because they are so young. Since we've gotten back together, I've just been enjoying the time he does spend with all of us, and not pressuring him for more. That seems to be working a lot better.

> "Josh and I once had a wonderful relationship, and I'm hoping that, as the children get older and he can relate to them better, we'll be close again. Till then, I'll enjoy what we do have and work toward making it better."

Penny has learned a new behavior pattern. By not getting into arguments with Josh about the amount of time he spends with the children, the time they do spend together is more enjoyable, a factor that encourages Josh to want to spend more time with his family.

During your time apart you've read, you've talked to friends, you may have taken workshops or gone into counseling in order to learn more effective ways of interacting. When you apply these methods and experience success, you gain the confidence to keep learning and trying new behaviors.

What to Do When Nothing Has Changed

What if problems have remained the same, improved only superficially, or even gotten worse? What do you do then? Idyllic as a reunion may seem, if the original problems are not well on the way to being resolved, you're going right back into the frying pan. No matter how much you love each other, the same fights and battles are going to erupt. If nothing has happened, you still have the same relationship that didn't work.

What will you do about it? Will you reunite, knowing that the same situation exists? "Honey, come back to me and we can work things out; I promise I'll stop drinking." Promises of change *after* the reunion are rarely fulfilled. Even if your partner means, or thinks he means, every word, don't count on things to change after you get back together if there hasn't been signifcant change before. Change takes more than words, it takes action; it also takes time. If the separation, painfully shocking as it was, did not cause change, your (or his) return certainly will not. Returning to the same situation completes the cycle in which you and your partner fall back into the same dysfunctional behaviors. Change is much harder when reunited than when apart. That's one of the reasons we keep suggesting that you use this separation time to regain your self-esteem and build your confidence.

If the situation does not change, you'll have to do a great deal of soulsearching. You may decide whether to settle for the old relationship, with its problems, or end the relationship.

Should You Compromise Your Values?

By this time, you know yourself much better than you did before the separation. You have identified what's important to you. You have also identified the problems in the relationship and decided which ones conflict with your values. Now you have to decide just how important those values are in reference to the relationship and whether you are willing to compromise on them or forego them entirely.

Few things are black and white. On many points, you and your partner will be able to work out adjustments so that the needs of both of you can be met. Yet, when it comes to your core values, to those things that define who you are and what you expect from life, you must be willing to be strong. If you insist on fidelity, you may have to pay the price right now of staying apart longer. If you want your partner back, you may have to pay the price of looking the other way and knowing he's being unfaithful. Such choices are not easy to make. Take your time and be sure that you understand the consequences fully.

How Much Are You Willing to Compromise?

"I always thought that if I found out my husband was cheating on me, it would mean the end," said Karen. "But when he actually headed for the door, I found out how much I was willing to compromise. I was eager for us to stay together and work through this. I had to find a way to go beyond infidelity, to heal, forgive, and move on in order to have Jim back."

Like Karen, you may have to rethink and come to terms with value-laden issues and determine if you can do what is necessary to reunite with your partner. Can you make a complete shift in the way you see things? Are you willing to do what it takes to go beyond the pain? For example, if your spouse was unfaithful, can you see infidelity as a symptom of a relationship that wasn't working, or as a misguided attempt to escape from a personal problem that your partner was experiencing? Will you dwell on the infidelity or the lack of companionship, and let it cost you the relationship? How often will you forgive and forget?

Can You Wait It Out?

Making change takes time. Suppose that you are absolutely unwilling to reunite while your partner is still gambling. Quitting is only the first step. He still will need to get help by attending Gamblers Anonymous or seeing a therapist who specializes in addictions. In addition, he probably needs financial counseling, a schedule of regular payments to his creditors, and perhaps employment counseling. All of these take time. You need to decide whether you are willing to reunite at the beginning of his program or prefer to wait until some measureable progress has been made. If your partner seems to be making a sincere effort or is actively seeking help, you may decide that good faith is enough and return. You may also want to join a support group for partners and families of addicts such a Alanon or Co-Dependents Anonymous in order to gain information and understand your role in the addiction process. Or you may decide to stay apart until he has been in recovery for six months or a year. Again, the choice is yours. Just be sure you make an informed choice.

Have You Reclaimed Your Life?

You've identified your values and set goals to get what you really want. Now you're determining whether you have come far enough and are stable enough to be ready for reconciliation at this time. You've considered whether the old problems have been resolved and what still needs to be done. You've decided what to do if little has changed. You've decided how much to compromise and on what. By now, you're recognizing that your decisions revolve around you and tie in with how much you understand yourself and what you want out of life. At this stage there are some very important questions to ask yourself.

Questions to Ask Yourself

Are you in control of your emotions now, rather than letting your actions control you? When you and your partner separated, regardless of who left whom or why, your life changed dramatically. Suddenly, the familiar routine was not the same. You might have found yourself avoiding friends, worried that they wouldn't want a "fifth wheel" around. Perhaps you stopped socializing as much or avoided familiar places because you didn't want to break into tears. You might have had difficulty at work. You probably spent more time than usual with your children, giving them support and drawing strength from them. Or, maybe you spent less time with them, even neglected them.

The little everyday activities that provided structure changed—perhaps drastically shattering the comfort of your life.

Things are different when you are suddenly "single" again, or a "single parent." At the beginning of the separation, your world was reeling. Now, the question is, are you on solid ground again? Have you regained your old routine, or built a new one that is comfortable for you? Have you regained your equilibrium and stabilized? One way to find out is to ask yourself the following questions.

1. Am I able to function day by day without emotional outbursts? Can I make it through a day without crying? Have I developed some internal self-control that allows me to face the world? Do I have a coping system that lets me manage even on the worst days?

2. Are my children doing okay? Have their lives gone back to normal as much as possible? Are they playing with their friends, getting their schoolwork done, dealing with the loss of their other parent? Are they able to talk about their father or mother without becoming emotionally upset?

3. Am I dealing well with my children? Have I learned not to criticize their father or mother in front of them? Am I refraining from expecting them to be my sole emotional support and not leaning on them more than they can handle? Am I trying to treat them the same way I did before the separation, being neither too strict nor too indulgent?

4. Am I letting my friends help me? Do I allow them to give me comfort and support in their own way, without resenting or demanding it? Do I allow myself to be vulnerable in front of them?

5. Do I help my friends? Am I back to equal friendships, giving (nearly) as much as I am taking? Am I thinking about them and their needs rather than only concentrating on my concerns? Am I willing to go out with couples

who are still together, and accept the possibility they love me for myself, not just as half of a couple?

6. Am I in good health, eating properly, sleeping well, exercising regularly? Am I taking care of myself, allowing me to pamper myself when necessary on those "blue" days?

7. Am I accepting occasional lapses such as the day I overdid the chocolates and skipped the aerobics? Do I allow myself to fail once in a while without being too hard on myself? Do I recognize that there are plateaus, and that I'm not a "bad person" if I don't improve for a while?

8. Am I in control financially? Have I changed my spending habits to reflect my new financial situation? Have I stopped splurging just to punish him (if he's paying the bills) or to make myself feel better? Am I living a lifestyle I can afford?

9. Am I planning my financial future wisely? Am I budgeting my money, balancing my bank account?

10. Is my job going well? Am I functioning at the same level I was before the breakup, or very close to it? Have my co-workers stopped giving me a little extra leeway because of my situation and begun expecting me to contribute as usual? Am I doing so? Have I settled back into the routine?

11. Am I back to planning for the future in my job? Am I looking forward to next week, next month, next year? Do I have work goals, things I am striving toward? Have I begun to look ahead?

12. Am I more self-reliant? Can I depend on myself? Do I deal with events in my life without feeling that I need to call on my partner or depending on my family? Do I respect myself and my abilities enough to be able to handle most situations most of the time?

13. Am I clear about what I want and need? Have I discussed my strengths and developed them? Do I have more self-confidence now than I did when we broke up?

These are all important questions, and you'll need to address them before you consider reconciliation. They're phrased so that the more "yes" answers you have, the more equilibrium you've regained, and the better your chances are of a successful reconciliation. Almost certainly there are a number of areas in which you are still unsteady, because regaining your equilibrium to the point where you are ready to reconcile takes time. If you go through these questions and feel that you are not sufficiently stable yet, you may want to reconsider an immediate reconciliation. It's vital that you be secure in yourself before you try to get back together. Just as you need time to recover and be strong if you've had a physical injury—you need time to recover from an emotional one. You want to go back into the relationship feeling secure that what you're doing is right for you.

And that's what your partner needs from you, too. Earlier in the book we discussed how your being overly dependent and clinging can actually drive your partner away. No one wants to shoulder the burden of someone else's emotional health—it will either frighten him away or give him a sense of power over you that can lead to problems later. Remember: No one can take power from you; only you can give it away. Once you have reached emotional equilibrium, you become more desirable in your partner's eyes as a person who is in control of her own life.

Susan found this out after twenty-one years of marriage. Susan had three grown children, a good home, and what she thought was a stable marriage until Robert began womanizing. Unable to cope with the betrayal of infidelity, she left her husband. Though immobilized at first, Susan in time renewed her priorities and reorganized her life. First, she moved to another state to be near her mother, whose health had begun failing. Although she had never worked outside the home before, she got a job and began a career. Along the way she became more confident and—in Robert's eyes—much more desirable. Four years later,

Robert decided it was Susan he wanted, and began wooing her again. She still loved Robert and took him back, this time with a greatly increased sense of self-respect and self-confidence. The two have begun a joint business and are devoted to each other. Susan has never been happier. As she puts it, "I got both the man I love, Robert, and the woman I love—me!"

When you start thinking of reconciliation, it's a time of hope and fear: hope that things will be better this time, fear that the destructive old patterns will reassert themselves.

If you've developed your confidence and self-esteem, put your priorities in order, and learned new ways of interacting, you have the ingredients of a successful reunion. Now that you know *you're* ready to reconcile, the question is whether you and your partner, as a couple, are ready to come back together again.

CHAPTER EIGHT

Are We Ready To Reconcile?

In the previous chapter, we focused on *you*, on how you were feeling about yourself and your goals, needs and desires. In this chapter, the focus shifts to the two of you together and the progress you each have made during the separation. In considering a reunion, remember that there are really three entities involved: you, your partner, and the relationship. Now it's time for both of you *together* to consider the relationship itself. When couples get back together, after a period of healing and growth, renewed relationships can be very special indeed. How can you determine if the *two of you* are really ready? What are the signs?

Why Did You Choose This Person?

Marcy and George

"I hope we can just enjoy ourselves tonight without getting into an argument," Marcy thought, as she and George got ready to spend an evening with friends Jessica and Michael. It was an evening they were both looking forward to, but as they were getting dressed, yet another of their now-too-frequent fights erupted. As Marcy later told Jessica, "George began picking on me again, as usual. He criticized my hairstyle, my makeup, my dress. He said that I had put on weight, and that I needed to shape up. It seems all he does these days is criticize. I didn't mind his comments so much when we were first married; it was even kind of flattering that he paid so much attention to how I looked, or what I did. But now, I resent it—I wish he'd find something else to focus on. We end up fighting all the time because nothing I do is ever good enough for him." Marcy's eyes swelled with tears. "I'm sure he doesn't love me anymore. In fact, the way he acts, I don't think he even likes me."

As the men moved outside to admire Michael's latest home improvement project, George spoke up angrily. "Marcy never asks my opinion anymore. She acts as if what I think doesn't matter. Whatever happened to the woman I married? She used to care a lot about what I thought. Now she couldn't care less." George paused, "Why doesn't she think about *me* sometimes? I think if she had to choose between me and that damn career of hers, I'd come out in second place!"

Do you sometimes feel that your needs have changed since you first entered your relationship or that they are no longer being met? Like Marcy and George, our needs are always changing. Although our core values usually remain the same, we change as we pass through the various stages of life and learn from our experiences. Each of us is always in some process of change—and so is your relationship.

Marcy

A sensitive youngster, Marcy felt awkward and was inclined to shyness as she grew up. Although she was attractive, she never felt so, especially in comparison to her older sister, Angela, who was vivaciously pretty and the center of attention. Marcy often remarked that when she was with Angela she felt invisible; no one paid much attention to her.

Marcy met George at a friend's wedding when she was twenty. She was pleased when George sought her out and asked for her phone number. He in turn was flattered by her attention and the way she deferred to him. Although not outwardly apparent, George felt that he didn't quite measure up to others' expectations, and tried to hide these feelings by displaying a super-confident attitude. He was gratified by Marcy's absorbed attention—and felt that he had finally found the right woman.

As Marcy and George started dating, they quickly fell into a pattern in which George made the decisions and Marcy went along with them. Where they went, who their friends were, and what they did were usually George's decisions. It wasn't that

Marcy lacked ideas or opinions, but rather that George seemed to be much happier taking the lead. However, two years after their marriage, Marcy's competence led to a promotion at the travel agency where she worked. She enjoyed her job organizing tour groups and hoped eventually to open her own agency. Marcy's increased responsibility led to a growing sense of self-confidence—it felt good to make her own decisions.

As Marcy's new-found independence carried over into her marriage, she requested George's opinion less frequently. She still casually asked, "Do you like it?" when she bought a new outfit, but showed little concern if George didn't. The final blow came when Marcy cut her long hair. George exploded. She knew how much he admired it. It seemed to symbolize everything that had gone wrong between them and triggered a major argument that left them both shaken. As time went on, Marcy became more outspoken and independent their fights became more frequent, and more serious. A year later, they separated.

Filled and Unfilled Needs

Marcy and George were wrestling with a problem that every couple faces—adjusting to the changing needs of the other person. No one is ever "still the same person" you married; our needs change over time. In this case, Marcy was once content with letting George make all the decisions without much regard for her preferences. As she became more independent, she was no longer willing to take a back seat, and this change was reflected in their marriage.

Everyone goes into a marriage or a relationship with special needs. One person may be looking for a feeling of belonging, another for security, still a third for companionship. In this case, Marcy had a great need for attention and approval. She wanted to feel that she was pretty and desirable, and she was gratified when George paid attention to her. It was flattering to have someone focus on her.

After their marriage, Marcy's earlier insecurity evaporated as she began developing more self-confidence through her work.

Marcy discovered that she was quite competent; she enjoyed making decisions and was good at managing people. Her growing self-confidence began to affect all aspects of her life, and she was less willing to look to George for guidance.

George

As George grew up, he was constantly compared unfavorably to his sister, who excelled academically and in sports and had many friends. George, in contrast, had difficulty with schoolwork and little ability in sports and was constantly belittled by his family for not measuring up. As he put it, "I was the kind of overweight kid that got called a 'nerd.' " He didn't find acceptance until he attended college, where he lost weight and discovered that a few drinks before a party made him feel considerably more at ease. When Marcy came into his life, her shyness and seeming dependence made him feel important and boosted his spirits.

"Marcy was wonderful at first," he said. "She was everything I ever wanted. She respected my opinion and acted as if she cared about what I thought. But since Marcy's promotion, everything has changed. She rarely bothers to ask me for suggestions; she just goes out and does what she wants. I don't think she cares about what I think any more—or about me, for that matter."

Like many of us, George had found security in someone else's dependence on him. It had propped up his own fragile ego. As long as Marcy needed him, he could feel strong and assured. But as Marcy started to gain confidence, she relied less on George, and he felt his position slipping.

George was hurt and angry when Marcy told him she felt suffocated in the relationship and resented his need for control. She said she wanted to leave and get some space for herself to find out what she was capable of. When Marcy moved out, George, who was desperate to save his marriage, went for counseling, hoping to find some way to bring her back. It took several sessions, during which he raged at Marcy's "self-centeredness and lack of commitment to the relationship," before he was able to acknowledge that he had a need to feel powerful and competent, a need which been filled by Marcy's former dependence.

Over the next few months, George began to work through old issues regarding his lack of self-esteem. He learned new behaviors and ways of thinking that bolstered his self-confidence. By using these new principles, he was able to start making friends and building a new social life for himself. He also enrolled in a course that would put him in line for promotion. Almost a year after their separation, George ran into Marcy at a supermarket. He invited her back to his apartment, and they spent a pleasant, relaxed evening, much like the ones they had before their problems started. As they parted, Marcy smilingly said, "Maybe you'd like to come over for dinner and see what I bought on my trips." After many months of going his or her own way, it was the start of a new relationship for them.

Marcy and George had found an important key to happiness: the realization that you cannot make another person fill your needs. Only *you* can fill your needs. When George and Marcy went off on their separate paths, building their own individual lives, they found they had the power to fulfill their individual needs. They came to the realization that no one else can make you happy; only you can make yourself happy. It was at that point that they were able to get back together again in a mutually satisfying relationship.

Identifying Your Needs

Most people's needs fit into one or more of these categories: physical, spiritual, emotional, intellectual, familial, financial. What about you and your partner? Regardless of whether you're separated, having trouble, or back together after having been apart, think about the needs you both brought into the relationship.

What Needs Did You Bring to the Relationship?

What were your needs when you got married? Some common needs are wanting to escape from your parents, wanting a mother/father for your children, fearing you couldn't find another partner because no one else would ask you, dealing with being pregnant, wanting more financial security, feeling left out because all your friends had gotten married, being lonely and wanting someone you could do things with, wanting children, feeling you didn't "belong" without being married, feeling you had never met anyone so exciting, wanting to "save" someone. There are many reasons that people enter relationships. What were *your* primary reasons?

Here's an exercise to help you identify the needs you had at the beginning of the relationship. Check them off with your comments and add more as you think of them. You may be surprised by what you find out about the needs you brought into the relationship.

EMOTIONAL NEEDS

_____   I was in love; I found my soulmate.

_____   My partner made me feel complete.

_____   I wanted a best friend, a companion.

_____   I was tired of dating.

_____   I wanted to improve my social standing in
               the community.

_____   I saw this as my last chance—I was afraid no one
               else would ask me to marry.

_____   My partner needed me.

_____   I wanted fun, excitement, new friends and adventures.

_____   I wanted the security of knowing someone
               was there for me.

_____   _____

PHYSICAL NEEDS

_____   I or my partner was pregnant.

_____   We had a great sex life; I felt fulfilled.

_____   My partner could take care of me physically/
               financially.

_____   We liked the same activities and sports.

_____   _____

SPIRITUAL NEEDS

_____   My partner shared my religious beliefs.

_____   My religious beliefs said that I couldn't have sex
without being married.

_____   My religious beliefs stressed the importance of
marriage and family.

_____   _____

FAMILIAL NEEDS

_____   I wanted children and a family of my own.

_____   I wanted to feel part of a family.

_____   I needed help taking care of my children.

_____   My family was pressuring me to get married.

_____   I wanted to get away from my family.

_____   My children needed another parent as a role model
and liked my partner.

_____   _____

FINANCIAL NEEDS

_____   I needed help paying the bills.

_____   I wanted a dual income to improve my lifestyle.

_____   I wanted to travel and do things I couldn't afford
on my income.

_____   I knew I could quit my job if I got married.

_____   I knew my partner could help me in my career.

_____   _____

INTELLECTUAL NEEDS

_____   My partner was mentally stimulating—we shared
                the same interests.

_____   My partner had the same educational background.

_____   My partner promised to to help further my education.

_____   I wanted to learn from my partner's expertise /
                knowledge.

OTHER (If you had additional reasons list them here. Try to be as specific as you can.)

_____   _____

_____   _____

_____   _____

What Needs Did Your Partner Bring to the Relationship?

Once you've completed this inventory, have your partner complete it also, if possible. Then discuss your mutual needs and how they have been fulfilled or have changed. If your partner is not available, complete the same inventory as if you were your spouse. Try to identify why your partner married you and what needs he expected you to fill. Think hard about this one; there may be reasons that you don't want to admit to yourself. Put yourself in your partner's shoes and try to see the relationship through his eyes.

What Needs Do You Have Now?

Now, look once more through the reasons why you came together. Look at the needs you checked. Were those needs met? Do you still have them? For some, the chief test is whether you still look to your partner to fill that need: **Would you come together/get married today because of it?** If the need is not strong enough to cause you to enter into a relationship again, consider it filled.

Each of us enters a relationship with our own special needs and expectations which are very real, even it they seem trivial or unimportant to our partner. Often people enter into a marriage or relationship believing their partner should fill their needs—and when the needs are not filled, they blame their partner for being insensitive or uncaring.

In a satisfying marriage, there is a balance between needs and expectations. Each partner is satisfied that important needs are being met. Problems start when there is a serious gap between what we actually receive from the relationship and what our expectations are. But as Eleanor Roosevelt said, "In time, each of us must discover that we can never really live anyone else's life—not your partner's, not even your own child's. You have to live your own life; you, and you alone, are responsible for you."

With that in mind, think about your needs at this time. A listing is provided below, with divisions into categories—physical, spiritual, emotional, intellectual, familial, and financial—to guide you. Write down your current needs. Be specific. For example, under familial, you might put "More time with my daughter." Take your time and come up with as complete a list as you can.

EXAMPLES OF BASIC NEEDS

CATEGORY	NEEDS
Physical	Food, shelter, clothing, sex, physical contact, exercise, safety, health care.
Financial	Financial security, comfort items, basic expenses cared for, money for fun things, savings for future and retirement.
Emotional	Love, commitment, emotional security, sharing, approval, understanding, recognition by peers, friendship, stability.

Familial	Marriage/partnership, children, closeness to family, commitment to common goals, good parental relationship, time with husband and children.
Intellectual	Educational growth, mental stimulation, stimulating discussion, cultural enjoyment (art/literature/music).
Spiritual	Spiritual belief, peace with self, concept of soul-mate, integrity, time for solitude, closeness to nature/outdoors.
Other	

Now think about how well each of your needs is being filled. Go back to your list and, next to each need, write down whether it is filled or not. You may find it helpful to "rate" each need by the percent it is filled. For example, now that you have a good job, the need for financial security may be 90% filled. Maybe your need for a best friend was 100% filled when you became close to someone at work or school. Maybe your need for approval was 50% filled when you got a promotion. How does your partner help fill these needs? Give yourself time to think about where you are *now* in your relationship and how you feel about your needs *now*.

Also, go back to Chapter Four and review the values you listed as important to you so that you are aware, when you and your partner begin speaking about reconciling, of how well they're reflected in the needs you have met.

What Needs Does Your Partner Have Now?

Now do the same thing for your partner. Look back over his needs at the time you first met and think about how they have changed. Then get another sheet of paper and list your partner's current needs. You may not be able to assess your partner's needs accurately, but use your best judgment. When you have completed the list, go back through it, and write down whether or not that need is filled. Best of all would be for you to do this together with your partner. You will each learn a great deal about what needs and expectations you are bringing to the relationship.

Once both of your needs have been aired and discussed, you'll discover a mixture of emotional needs ("I need trust and intimacy") and practical needs ("I need to have you take over more of the responsibilities of child-rearing and give me some time off").

In doing this exercise together, you'll get to know each other better, and the information you both gain will help you decide whether "we," the two of you as a couple, are ready to get back together. When you understand each other's needs, those with deep emotional roots, and the more day-to-day needs, you have a good start toward resolution and reunion.

You may discover that your partner has a need you cannot live with; for example, the freedom to spend several nights out alone each week. In that case, the time is not right for reconciliation unless he changes those patterns or you can make major compromises in your values. If you have a new need that he finds disconcerting, such as spending more time at work because of a promotion, you need to discuss whether he can accommodate it in order to give your reconciliation the best chance.

In all these activities you have probably discovered more about yourself and the kind of person you are. That knowledge is essential in building a strong, intimate relationship. Discovering what went wrong, how the relationship gradually disintegrated, and what changed is necessary to make it strong and healthy again. Your partner may or may not have done this. Either way, this is the time to determine what each of you brought to the relationship and what expectations and behaviors contributed to its disintegration. The separation period has provided each of you with the opportunity to see things from a clearer perspective so that positive change can take place.

How Well Did Your Relationship Meet Your Needs?

The next thing for the two of you to discuss is how your relationship, as you knew it before, did or did not meet your needs. Now is your chance to be specific. Probably you were not quite as clear on your needs while you were going through the pain of slipping apart. There were too many emotions to think clearly. You might have felt your needs strongly but not have been able to articulate them. We all expect our partners to be mindreaders ("If he really loved me, he'd know what I want!"), but needs have to be specified. During the separation you've had the time to step back and look at yourself, to analyze who you are and what you want. Now you can express your desires and listen to your partner express his.

When George and Marcy were able to sit down and talk, they found out that one of his needs hadn't been met by their old relationship. In fact, there hadn't even been an attempt to meet it because there was no awareness of the strength of the need.

"I was amazed to hear George say that he wanted me to spend more time with his friends and family. I knew that he resented my working so much, but I thought that was because I was always tired. Now I've changed my schedule so that we have more time for social activities together."

Marcy knew that the relationship had not met her primary need, even though she expressed it directly and often. "I kept telling George that I needed more praise for my accomplishments. It wasn't any fun coming home if George shrugged things off. I told him that, when we get back together, I want to get more compliments and stroking."

George understands. "Marcy did tell me I was too critical of her and didn't give her enough praise. Now that I understand her need and how strong it is, I'm going to tell her how much I love her and how proud I am of her."

Marcy and George illustrate two common dilemmas. For George, the old relationship was not meeting a need because the need had not been expressed. For Marcy, the old relationship was not meeting a need, even though it had been clearly stated. In discussing their needs, both partners agreed that they could work together to fulfill them. In order to have a successful reconciliation, you and your partner should be able to fulfill, or find compromises on, your most important needs.

Go through your needs one by one, and be candid about how the old relationship did or did not meet them. Avoid vague generalities or accusatory statements, such as "You never praised me." Instead, be as specific as you can—for example, "I really wanted you to congratulate me when I won the Employee of the Month award for working on the Baranko contract, and I was disappointed and hurt when you didn't." A generality doesn't tell your partner what you want; a specific example lets him know in terms he can act on.

How Have You Both Changed?

If you have used your separation time constructively, you will have developed more self-respect and self-confidence. You may also have changed in external ways. You may have gotten a new job, made new friends, taken up a new hobby, or enrolled in classes. Let your partner know that you are not the same person you used to be, and ask him to share with you how he has changed. Also discuss how the changes have affected each of you. The following are some questions to help you and your partner get started talking about the changes. These can also be used as "stepping stones" to the deeper, more emotional issues.

1. How have my daily habits changed? Have I changed my sleep hours, meal times, or other routine activities?

2. What new activities have I begun? Do I have new sports, hobbies, clubs? Have I begun taking classes?

3. What's going on at work? Have I gotten a promotion, a new project, new co-workers?

4. What's happened in my relationship with the children? What are we doing that we didn't do before? Am I seeing more of them or less? Am I treating them dif-

ferently? What are my children's needs at this time? How has the separation affected them? What is their relationship with the absent partner?

5. How has my social life changed? Have I made new friends? Am I spending more/less time with old friends? What am I doing for fun these days?

6. What strengths and weaknesses have I discovered since the separation? What most surprised me about myself—something I never thought I could do, but did? What areas do I wish I could be stronger in?

7. What fears did I have during the separation? How did I handle them? What did I learn from them?

8. How do I feel about myself since the separation? How did my self-concept change during the months we were apart? Was there any one time when I felt myself changing? How?

9. What do I realize about my partner that I didn't realize before? How did my time apart make me understand him more? In what ways have my feelings toward him changed?

10. What do I realize about the relationship that I didn't realize before? How did the separation force me to view it in a new light? What did I learn?

11. If I were starting my marriage all over again, what would I do differently?

12. What did I most want to tell my partner on those long nights we were apart?

13. Have my partner and I been talking to each other openly and honestly? Do we treat each other with respect? Has communication improved? Are we able to talk about our needs, fears, past hurts, future dreams?

14. Have we both grown in awareness? Do we have better insights about what went wrong before, and ways to avoid that in the future?

15. Do we avoid blaming each other? Have we learned to listen with our hearts as well as our ears?

16. Are we building trust and intimacy? Do we have a new history of interactions that support the relationship?

17. Are we having fun together? Do we enjoy each other's company? Can we laugh together?

18. Could we be friends? Do my partner and I genuinely like each other as people? Are we companions as well as lovers?

These questions will help both of you discover your innermost feelings, as well as the changes that have taken place. You'll gain a better idea of the areas where you've grown and where your needs match and mismatch. Marcy and George had completely different reactions to the separation, but they both ended up learning a great deal about themselves, and growing. When they got together to talk, they were surprised and pleased at the changes the other had gone through. Marcy never thought that George, who looked so strong, could be so vulnerable; George was amazed that Marcy had so much confidence. When you and your partner discuss your changes, you will probably be pleasantly surprised as well. Remember, your partner may have dealt with his pain in a completely different manner.

Marcy: "I withdrew into my shell when George and I separated. I didn't want to talk to anyone, or be with anyone. I just went to work, then came home and flopped down in front of the television set. I spent most of my time thinking. I wrote for hours in a journal, trying to analyze my feelings. I changed in that I understand myself more, and have much greater confidence in my abilities."

George: "I did just the opposite. When Marcy left me, I went crazy. I acted like a kid. I spent money like mad on a new car, new stereo system, new clothes. I did anything that would take my mind off what was happening. I even tried to get into another relationship, but I just couldn't make a go of it. My change took me a lot longer than Marcy's. I didn't really enjoy the freedom. I realized that I wanted a one-to-one relationship—and that I wanted it with Marcy."

Marcy: "I found out I was stronger than I thought. Once I finally came out of my shell, I made new friends and discovered that other people thought I had a lot to offer. After George's always putting me down, that was like music to my ears, and I thrived on it."

How Will These Changes Affect Your Relationship?

You discussed how the previous relationship did or did not fulfill your needs. Also discuss how your new relationship will handle the changes that have taken place. For example, if you have gotten a new job that demands more of your time, how will that affect the relationship? If a promotion has made more money available, how will you spend it? If your partner has started spending more time with children from a previous marriage, how can that time be incorporated in your new relationship? Exploring the ways in which the relationship will be different, and how you will handle the changes, can help you decide whether the time is right to reconcile.

You both bring old issues back into the relationship, many with roots that go deep into your past. Now you have an opportunity to rebuild your relationship and design the one you wanted all along. If there are unfinished issues that affect your individual peace of mind, discuss them with your partner.

Are Your Needs the Same Now?

You've been looking at your needs, deciding how important they are and which have been filled. In order to clarify your relationship, it's important to consider whether your and your partner's needs are compatible. For example, do you need more independence, while your spouse needs someone to be dependent on him? While compromise and adjustment are necessary in any relationship, if your needs and those of your partner are fundamentally different, it may not be possible for either of you to get what you want without causing serious discomfort to the other, unless you are able to find creative solutions. Can you resolve your differing needs? Suppose you married for fun and excitement or to get away from what you saw as a dead end life on your own, yet your spouse has a job that demands most of his time. You don't get to travel, he's too tired in the evenings to go out, and he works on the weekends. You feel bored and dissatisfied. Obviously, the need for excitement is unfilled. If this is still important to you, can you live without it? Are you willing to try new approaches? How can you get this need met without your partner, yet without putting a strain on the relationship?

These are not simple questions. Finding solutions and working out compromises requires thought. How important is a certain need to you? Will not having it filled create a serious dissatisfaction in your life? Was that need a primary reason you entered the relationship in the first place? Imagine that you met someone new today who is everything you want except for fulfilling that one particular need. Would you pursue the relationship?

No one can answer these questions but you (although a therapist can help you discover your priorities). If things are not going to change, are you able to accept that and continue in this relationship? Are there other ways you can fill your needs? Keep in mind that the same questions apply to your partner as well. Will he be willing to accept unfilled needs? How important are they to him? If he sees that you will never be the one to help him fill them, will he stay with you or find other ways to get them met?

Everyone has needs that are real and important. We choose our partner seeking to meet them. During the relationship, our needs may be completely fulfilled; they may be partly fulfilled; or they may be completely unfulfilled. What's important right now is that you each identify your needs and work toward finding ways to satisfy them. The values you listed in Chapter Four can

serve as a guideline for both of you to identify what you really
need for your happiness.

Caution! Wait Until You Can Both *Commit to the Relationship*
If either of you feels pushed or coerced into reconciliation, the
chances of working it out this time are poor. There will be resentment, anger, and the feeling that one person has manipulated the
other into a choice that wasn't mutual. The same problems that
separated you in the first place will arise again. There's always
the possibility that the ambivalent person will not give the
needed effort to make the relationship succeed. He may even
make sure that it doesn't. When Susan learned that her husband,
David, had stopped seeing the woman with whom he had been
having an affair, she pleaded for him to move back home. "See, I
told you it wouldn't work," David said, six weeks after they
reconciled. David came home, but wasn't committed to creating a
good relationship with his wife. In fact, he had yet to deal with
the demise of his failed relationship with his lover.

Can We Be a Couple Again?

You've analyzed both your needs, and how they were and were
not met by your relationship. You considered how you both have
changed, and how that would affect a renewed relationship. In
discussing these changes, remember the things you love in your
partner that made all this work worthwhile. Remind each other
of the good times and shared dreams: how you first met, the first
time you said "I love you," your joy when your children were
born, the look on the grandparents' faces when they held the
baby for the first time, the little things that demonstrated love, the
shared secrets that made you meet each other's eyes and smile.
Tell your partner what you respect and admire; what accomplishments you boast about to your friends; remind each other of
shared accomplishments. Recognize the parts of your life that
work well together. There is a lot of shared history between you
that is joyous. Find the bond between you and cherish it.

During the time you've been apart, you've had an opportunity to find your own identity and see your relationship from a new perspective. You've talked with others, read, and gained insights about causes of the problems and possible solutions. If you've been using this book as a guide, you have probably already started to institute changes. Perhaps you've started an exercise program to release some of your stress; maybe you've gone back to school or enrolled in a class to develop a long-standing interest. You may have started to build a new circle of friends whose interests more closely reflect yours. Perhaps you've become more involved in your work as a way of distracting yourself from pain about the relationship, or you may have started in counseling with a therapist. Continue doing these things when you reconcile. They are the things that have made you strong and given you a sense of self. They will continue to be valuable to you when you and your partner reconcile.

CHAPTER NINE

Now That You're Back Together:
How to Avoid the Pitfalls of Reconciliation

You have made a conscious decision to save your relationship. It's taken a lot of work and effort to reach this point. You recognized that it was first necessary to strengthen yourself and to revitalize and nurture your own personal growth. You committed yourself to a constructive plan of action to love your way back into the relationship. You and your partner are back together now, learning to be with each other in new ways. You're excited about being reunited and are enjoying the good times. Yet somewhere in the back of your mind there's a small voice that won't leave you alone. It keeps whispering things like, "What if he leaves again? What if I have to go through all that pain again? What makes me think that this is going to last?" Lingering doubts can make you feel insecure even at the best of times. Right now, when you're most vulnerable, even though you try to ignore them, they probably won't go away.

These feelings are a natural part of the coming-together process. You have high hopes and rosy expectations for the new relationship, which neither of you may be able to completely fulfill at this time. You may expect an unrealistic degree of change on the part of your partner, but growth is a continuous process.

You may also demand too much of yourself. You've worked very hard on becoming more self-aware during your time apart. You are justifiably proud of the progress you have made and feel much more confident in your ability to handle the relationship. However, don't expect yourself suddenly to be able to take care of everything that comes along. Have your expectations, dream the dreams, but root them in reality.

The Ups and Downs of Reconciliation

What can you expect, now that you are back together? You know that everything won't be perfect; how can you deal with the days when things seem to be falling apart? Here is an overview of some of the most common problems newly reconciled couples have and suggestions for handling them.

1. *Refusal to Deal with the Past*

Frances and Paul had been married for what Frances called "four of the most glorious years of my life." Then Paul began to have business problems that caused him to become sullen and withdrawn. Things became so bad that their marriage became, in Frances' words, "a nightmare," which led to separation.

After several months, during which they kept in touch, Paul abruptly did a complete reversal. He left his former business, dropped some acquaintances who had caused him trouble, and changed back to his former loving and affectionate self. One afternoon he appeared at Frances' door and told her he was ready to "pick up where we left off."

Frances was thrilled to have Paul back. However, she became intensely frustrated when he refused to discuss the reasons for his previous actions toward her. As far as he was concerned, "I'm back; let's leave it at that." The more Frances tried to talk about their former problems, the more Paul withdrew. Finally, afraid of losing Paul entirely, Frances let the matter drop. But she felt very unhappy that Paul was denying her the opportunity to talk about their problems and their marriage.

While you were apart, you talked about your relationship to your friends, your family, your therapist, just about anyone who would listen. You couldn't wait to get back together with your partner and discuss things openly. Many times you said, "If only we could sit down and really communicate, everything would be so much better." During the reconciliation process, the two of you did open up, and have those heart-to-heart talks about the issues most important to you. You both gained a greater understanding from those conversations.

But now that you are living together again, things may be different. Perhaps you still want to talk about intimate feelings, but your partner does not. Many men are uncomfortable with intense discussions. They may be more willing to communicate openly during the separation, recognizing that it takes communication to solve the problems and get back together. Now that you are reunited, your partner may feel that there is no need to talk. After all, he reasons, why bring up the past and all its pain again?

This may really be frustrating for you. On the surface, it's difficult to argue with "Let's focus on the positive; let's not keep talking about the negative." It sounds so rational. Yet, the issues that concern you may still feel unresolved. There's no one magical moment in which your heart says, "Okay, that's it. We've now talked about the crisis long enough, and I am officially healed." Everyone heals at a different pace. Your spouse may be perfectly content with the new state of affairs and not need further discussion. You, on the other hand, may still be looking for explanations, so that you can understand what happened.

Your partner may be frustrated as well. He honestly feels that everything that needs to be said has been said. He can't understand why you keep going over and over the same things. He may even begin to resent your continuing efforts to talk about the past when he wants to focus on the present. In Chapter Six we explained how different processing styles can interfere with communication and gave reasons why your partner may not feel the need to express himself as fully as you do. If he has difficulty exploring a particular issue, use the skills of good communication to make improvement in this area possible. If you have a greater need to explore past issues than your partner does, consider finding an outlet in a support group, which also provides learning through shared experiences. A therapist can also help you gain perspective.

2. Fear Of Arguments

A second common problem during the reconciliation is the fear of fighting. Everything is going so well now, you reason. Your partner is back, you're in love again, things should be perfect. So when he does something that upsets you, you gloss over it and find excuses, or you harbor it and resent him without sharing the fact that you're upset. After all, the last thing you want to do is start another fight. You may be afraid that even the smallest argument might escalate into a major upheaval which would result in his leaving again.

Yet you can't just gloss over problems. Perhaps doing that is what led to the deterioration of your relationship in the first place. If you let the small irritations grow into larger ones, you eventually explode—or you hold the feelings inside you and let your resentment out in indirect ways. Unexpressed anger starts a dangerous cycle in which you hold your partner responsible for things that he doesn't even know are bothering you.

> One source of conflict between Frances and Paul before their separation was continuous fights over how little time Paul spent with the family. Paul felt that he was giving as much of himself as he could and that it was unreasonable to expect more. A few months after Frances and Paul reunited, Frances again asked Paul to spend more time at home. When Paul showed signs of annoyance ("You're not going to start that old beef again, are you, just when things are going so well?") Frances backed off immediately. She had no intention of causing a blow-up at this stage.
>
> Yet she knew that she had compromised her principles. Frances felt strongly that Paul should spend more time with his family and started to question just how committed Paul truly was. Because she had allowed him to cut off a discussion because of her fear it would turn into a fight, a very important matter went unresolved. What Frances could have done was let Paul know that even though he wasn't prepared to discuss it with her at that time, the matter was critical to her and something that they needed to resolve.

3. *Fear That the New Relationship Will Fail*

"For the first few months after Paul came back, I didn't withdraw my petition for divorce. I didn't go forward with it either. I thought that since Paul had changed so much in the six months before the separation, I had no way of knowing that he wouldn't change again. It seemed as if everything had happened overnight, as if I went to bed with my husband and woke up with a stranger. I was afraid that Paul might change that quickly again.

"As much as I loved Paul, I had to face the reality of the situation. I couldn't dismiss it as easily as he seemed to. Sure, Paul came back, but he could leave again at any time. I know I let this nervousness rule me for several months. It wasn't until we had been together again for about three months that I dropped the divorce suit. Luckily for me, Paul was willing to wait. He told me we were back together for life and the separation was just a bad memory. I think it was his utter certainty about the permanence of our relationship, more than anything else, that finally convinced me."

Once burned, twice shy. Even though you love your partner and have been longing for the time you would be back together with him, deep down inside of you there may be something holding you back—something that keeps you from giving your all. You just don't think you could go through all that pain again or survive those long nights alone, and you're terrified of putting yourself in a position to be hurt.

Wanting to succeed yet wanting to protect yourself can create serious problems. On the one hand, it's natural to be afraid of something that has the potential to hurt you deeply. On the other, you have to commit to the relationship totally in order to make it work. Not committing allows you to say, "I knew it wouldn't work out; I was right to hold something back," but it also sabotages the very thing you want most—a successful reunion.

Remember that your partner is also feeling insecure right now. He probably feels the same anxiety that you do—or even more, if he is the one who left. He may be thinking, "It's her turn now; when is she going to leave me?" Or he may feel that since he hurt you so badly, it's only a matter of time until you realize that he's not good enough for you. The key is not to let negative feelings and fears overwhelm you and the new love you have.

4. *Lack of Trust*

"When Paul and I were apart, he went out with his former girlfriend, a woman he had dated before we were married. I couldn't stop thinking of the two of them laughing, having sex, maybe discussing our marriage. How can I make love with Paul again, knowing he cheated on me? My rational mind tells me that it wasn't cheating, that we were separated, and that I was the one who had filed for divorce. But my heart still feels betrayed.

"I can't seem to trust Paul the way I used to. When he's late coming back from the office, I wonder whether he's with her. When he looks at a woman, I wonder whether he would ask her out if he weren't with me. I don't think it's jealousy, exactly; it's just that I don't trust him anymore. I used to enjoy it when other women looked at Paul. He's a very handsome man, and it made me proud to be with him and have other women checking him out. But now, when they look, I cringe. I don't feel secure that I'm the only one now."

It takes time to build trust into a relationship. Ideally, love and trust grow together, with trust being the strong foundation on which love is built. But events before and during the separation often shatter that trust. It may have been a secret you confided when you felt especially close that was later used against you. It may have been infidelity, or something done intentionally to hurt you. Whatever the action that caused its breakdown, now that you are together again, trust must be rebuilt.

5. *Lingering Rage and Resentment*

"If I'm supposed to be so happy, why do I feel angry all the time?" is a heartfelt question asked by many reunited couples. Everything was supposed to be better now that your partner's back, especially if he's being more tender and affectionate or doing thoughtful little things, trying to make up for the pain he's caused. He may be making an effort to make you happy, yet you may be feeling anger and resentment.

When you come back together, it's the happy ending in which you are naturally expected to be happy. Your friends congratulate you, your co-workers tell you they knew all along that things would work out, and your family heaves a sigh of relief. Yet you may wonder why you feel angry or let down instead of blissful.

Perhaps all is well at first, when lovemaking with a new passion keeps you feeling warm and fulfilled. But then you begin to focus on the past pain. "How could he have done this to me? How could he have hurt me this way? How could he have hurt our children? How could he make a fool of me, a mockery of our marriage?" Little by little, all the pain that you felt turns to anger and then to rage.

Frances felt her anger grow in the first few weeks that Paul was back. In their quiet moments, when they were at dinner or watching television, she would sometimes look at him and think, "How could you have been so hateful to me in these past months? How could you have consciously set out to destroy our marriage? How could you have treated our love so carelessly, even trying to drive me away?" The intensity of her rage surprised and frightened her. She didn't want to be angry; she wanted to use all her energies to be loving and warm and supportive of the new relationship. She wanted to nurture it like a newborn baby. But the rage would flare up without provocation. When she was cooking, she would suddenly be overwhelmed with anger at how Paul had refused to take her calls while they were separated. When she was driving to work, she would feel her stomach tighten as she thought of the pain she had experienced knowing of his infidelity. Her anger was threatening to overwhelm her.

Perhaps the worst part of rage is that it leaves you feeling guilty. You don't want to be angry all the time. You tell yourself that you "should" be happy, and you feel guilty about being angry. This may fuel your anger even further. You fear that if you express yourself, you're going to cause problems in the new relationship and sabotage it before it's had a chance to grow strong. Yet you can't help your feelings. As the rage wells up, all you can think about is what he put you through. You need to express this anger. If you can express it to your partner and have him understand that it's not directed at him now but at the situation that previously existed, all the better. A couples' support group where both of you can be assisted to process your feelings can be very helpful, as can a therapist whc can facilitate the release of your anger and help you deal with it.

6. *When the Second Honeymoon Ends*

When Paul began spending more time at work and less with Frances, she got nervous. "It was Paul's shutting me out of his life that caused all our problems before. Now, when he leaves for work before I'm even up, I think that he doesn't care as much. When he won't take a Saturday off to walk along the beach with me, as he did when we first got back together, I'm concerned that he doesn't want our relationship to work as much as I do. He tells me he's just busy and not to be silly or worry, but I can't help it. After all, I'm taking time out of my day to do things for him, and I'm just as busy as he is."

When you first get back together, you are usually both on your best behavior—doing little things to please the other and refraining from annoying habits that drive your partner up the wall. It's almost as if you are dating again. You spend time together doing amusing things, enjoying the relationship, and basking in your new-found love. It's like a second honeymoon.

The honeymoon stage isn't permanent, however, and little by little, as things start to wind down and you both become more secure in your reunion, it's natural to start being more relaxed. You might become a little less attentive, a little less supportive. Perhaps your partner buries himself behind the newspaper again, or you renew some of those irritating habits, like always being late. Does this mean the romance is gone? No. It means that the relationship has stabilized and that you are comfortable with each other. It's impossible to maintain artificial "dating" behavior for long; if your relationship is strong, you learn to accept each other's foibles.

When you reunite, it's easy to say that you will find ways to spend more time together and show your appreciation for each other. But often those little loving gestures become fewer in number and time spent together shrinks as the outside world starts to demand more attention. Perhaps you still want to spend more time with your partner, and he is now "too busy" for you. It's easy to feel insecure when you are still doing thoughtful things for him, yet your partner has gone back to—as you see it—taking you for granted. At such times, you may fear that the reunion didn't work and you may need to talk about ways to keep the romance and intimacy going.

How to Make Sure It's Better This Time

There are a number of ways that you can keep vitality and romance in your relationship. They are very much like the steps you took to bring you and your partner back together again. In Chapter Ten, we'll discuss how to sustain your relationship in greater detail. The points below are especially important during the early stages of reconciliation.

1. *Keep the Communication Going*
Communication is the key factor at this point in the renewal of your relationship. You're both experiencing many fears and apprehensions. You may be afraid to express them, meet with resistance from your partner about discussing them, or find that you both back off from talking at a deeper level. However, in order to establish or maintain intimacy, the open communication which started during the reconciliation process must continue.

Read Chapter Six with your partner, practice the skills of good communication, invite him to share his feelings, and listen—or get outside help. The degree to which you can communicate openly will determine the success of the reconciliation.

2. *Focus on the Present*
You have absolutely no power over the past. No matter how much you think, hope, and pray, you are not going to change one

minute of what has already happened. But you have a great deal of power over today, because you decide what you are going to do, say, think, and feel.

Many couples use a simple but powerful phrase to help them stay focused on the feelings and goals they're working toward: "One Day at a Time." Clear your mind of past events and the pain and unhappiness you went through, and focus only on the present. When you're feeling anxious, you ask yourself "What can I do *right now*?"

Of course, putting the past behind you is easier said than done. But there is an effective and fairly simple way to start. Listen to yourself, and be aware of what you are thinking and saying. You may not be conscious of how much you may be dwelling in the past. But when you begin to talk about it, stop! Make an effort to catch yourself. If you start to say, "When John left me, I . . ." Stop! Take a deep breath, and begin again. "Today I can . . . ." Today is all that matters.

Second, replace the past in your thoughts with something else. Refocus yourself. When that image of him with his former girlfriend flashes into your mind, replace it with the look on his face when he came toward you with his arms open, ready for a big hug. Instead of thinking of those nights apart, remember how wonderful it was the last time you were together. Plan a future.

3. *Continue to Take Care of Yourself*
During the separation stage, you worked at taking care of yourself. Continue to do so! Keep to that exercise plan, continue the classes you started. Just because your partner is back is no reason to stop caring for yourself. In order to have the best possible relationship, you want to be the best possible you.

4. *Keep Your New Life, as Well as the Old*
Remember your other commitments, and don't make your relationship the only important thing in your life. Of course you want to spend more time with your partner now, but don't make him the sole focus of your life. Continue to cherish the good friends who stood by you or the new friends you made during

the separation. The temptation, upon reunion, is to think that you have gotten everything you want and that you can let go of those "stop-gap measures" you took, such as getting together with friends or taking classes. Not so! Merge the best of the old with the best of the new. While you were apart, you probably set new goals for yourself. Keep working toward them.

5. *Consider Counseling, Individually and as a Couple*
If you were in counseling during the separation, now is not the time to quit. Continue your sessions. You'll have new, exciting, frustrating, and sometimes painful experiences to discuss, which a therapist can help you understand and work through. If your spouse is willing, get him into counseling with you. The two of you are taking those first steps to learning new ways of relating to each other. A professional who is skilled and objective, can be of immense help at this time.

You struggled a long time to get to this point. But happy endings are only the beginning. Some of the problems that were there before the separation may still remain; others may have arisen. You can resolve some of the predictable frustrations you are likely to undergo. Remember, they are a natural part of reconciliation.

Now that your reconciliation is off to a good start, it's time to look at how to sustain a loving and lasting relationship.

CHAPTER TEN

Sustaining a Loving and Lasting Relationship

The next time you go to a restaurant, look around. You will probably see at least one couple that just *looks right* together. They may not be talking much, yet you sense that they enjoy each other's company. All of us want something like that. When we fantasize about our future as half of a couple, we imagine the closeness of loving and being loved in return.

Both you and the relationship have been through a lot and have come out stronger. As you learned in the last chapter, however, it's important to keep learning and growing. Your relationship needs constant care and nurturing. Even though it's much stronger than before, it still needs continued attention. What are the keys to sustaining a loving and lasting relationship? The most important is to make a commitment to the relationship. Other important elements are communication, maintaining your own identity, scheduling fun into your marriage, investing time in the relationship, developing a strong support system that's rooting *for* the relationship, continued reading and learning, cherishing your love, appreciating what you've worked so hard to get, anticipating the good times ahead, developing tolerance, and being friends.

ONE: Commit Yourself to the Relationship

This is the most important point. Keep the relationship and its well-being foremost in your mind. Think in terms of how your decisions and interactions will affect the relationship as well as both of you as individuals. You may feel that you individually can survive poor communication, too little time spent together, or lack of fulfillment in areas of need. But can the relationship survive? The relationship has to be your number one priority if it is to succeed.

When problems come up, sit down and discuss how they affect the relationship. Too often, conflicting needs or expectations are seen as win/lose struggles between partners. "If you get your way, I don't get mine." Instead, think of making the relationship the winner and ask, "How will what we're doing affect our relationship?"

"I had to ask for a transfer to another office," Tom said, "even though Carol believed me when I said it was all over between me and the woman I had been seeing. It just caused her too much pain to know that I'd still be in daily contact with her. When we looked at what that constant strain would do to the relationship, we decided it wasn't worth it. Our relationship comes first."

TWO: Keep the Lines of Communication Open

The many couples whose histories of successful reconciliation form the basis for this book had problems as different as they were. Their ways of coping with them covered the spectrum. Yet one thing they all had in common was a strong belief that the most important factor in successfully reuniting and sustaining a loving and lasting relationship was their emphasis on good communication. Time and again they told us, "Don't let the problems build up. Make time, every day, to share what's going on in your life. Don't talk just about the big serious topics, but about the little day-to-day ones too. Express yourself clearly. No one is a mind reader; don't assume the other person knows what you're thinking. Talk, listen, and face the problems. They won't go away if you ignore them, they'll just get worse!"

Good communication is a two-way street. It requires listening skills as well as the ability to state your needs clearly and in a way that will help your partner understand you. Active listening brings couples closer together. Carol and Tom came back together after a particularly rough separation. Tom had dated quite a bit, including several women Carol knew and one business associate who worked in the same office. Carol had a lot of insecurities and concerns about her husband's fidelity and asked that Tom discuss them with her. Tom felt that if Carol had more information about what was going on in his business life and felt more a part of it, she would be less anxious.

"I told Carol more about what I do and the highlights and frustrations of my day. As she got to know the people in my office, she felt closer to them and less threatened. What happened was that, as I began to share more of my day with her, I felt closer to Carol and she needed less reassurance about other women and felt more trust in me."

"In the beginning, I mostly listened while Tom talked about his day," Carol said. "But the talking carried over into other areas as well. It was as if once Tom learned how to talk about work, he was willing to go the next step and discuss other things, too. We talk about everything now, getting problems out into the open before they become really bad."

Communication is as much an attitude as a skill. When you have the desire to communicate, not just to talk *at* each other but *with* each other, your level of intimacy grows.

THREE: Develop and Maintain Your Own Identity

You have to find meaning outside of your partner, no matter how much you love him, in order to be a complete human being, an individual in your own right, who is able to bring more to the relationship. When you are strong and more fulfilled, you also become more interesting, and have more to share. You are more intriguing to your partner, as he finds that you have a lot more to offer than he ever suspected.

You worked on gaining a sense of identity, on knowing who you are and what you want, during the separation. Now that you know yourself better, cherish that knowledge and continue to build on it. Find your own focus and keep it sharp. You set goals for yourself during the time apart; continue to work toward them now. Your partner will respect you for doing so, and respect is one of the foundations of any strong relationship.

Each of you should be independent and yet interdependent. Be certain that you have a life of your own, that you could survive apart if you had to. Knowing that you have that option gives much more meaning to your decision to be together. Now you are together not out of desperation, not because you have to be, but because you want to be.

> "When Bob left me, my standard of living really fell," Carol said. "I had been pretty casual about my job because Bob was doing so well. We really didn't need my money. I used it mostly for extras and clothes. I enjoyed my work and the people around me, but I never took it seriously. I just figured Bob would always be there to take care of me. When he left, I had a pile of bills and a condo that used up most of my paycheck. I had to take in a roommate to make ends meet. It really shook me up, and I decided I would never let myself get that dependent again. I started digging into my job and found out what I would have to do to advance. I've gotten one raise and I'm due for another. Now that I know I can take care of myself, I feel a lot better about our relationship. I know I don't *need* Bob, I *love* him. When we got back together, and started talking about remodeling our house, I felt that my say really meant something."

FOUR: Lighten Up and Have Fun!

Put the fun back into your marriage! Remember all the silly little things that made you laugh when you first started dating? The spontaneous phone calls, the humorous cards, the impromptu dancing to the stereo? A relationship is not all heartfelt talks and serious moments. Part of the joy of being together is having fun. All too often, a couple focuses on the work and obligations and loses the vibrancy that kept the relationship alive. Fun is the lifeblood of marriage. It creates those special moments between you and your partner that sustain you through the inevitable rough spots. Be sure to take time for fun as regularly as you schedule work commitments or other obligations.

> "One of the reasons I fell in love with Carol was her sense of humor," Bob said. "She was always laughing, always having a good time. When we got back together again, I told her how much I missed being able to laugh with her. We both agreed that we needed more fun in our marriage and began including it. My idea of fun is surprises and silly jokes. I show up to take her to lunch when she doesn't expect it. Carol's idea of fun is a little more structured. She loves to look forward to things. She'll schedule an activity a month in advance and enjoy anticipating it. We've been having a good time, and it's brought us closer together. One of the reasons I love being with Carol is that we always have so much fun together."

FIVE: Invest Time in the Relationship

One of the most important factors in regaining intimacy and strengthening and sustaining a relationship is time. It takes time to learn to communicate well. It takes time to have fun together. It takes time just to be together. And time is the one element in our lives that is finite. You can make more money. You can move to a bigger house. You can acquire more friends, more possessions, more of anything you can name, except time. Time is constant. Everyone has the same twenty-four hours, seven days, fifty-two weeks. How time is allotted says a lot about how much you and your partner value each other. If your partner refuses to spend time on the relationship, you probably feel cheated and unappreciated. If he would rather spend a few more hours at work than with you, you feel that you have a lower priority. When he is willing to devote more time to you, he is telling you that you're important to him, that you're Number One.

Sustaining a loving and lasting relationship means that you're willing to commit yourself to sharing your time. It doesn't require huge investments; you can often create the same intimacy with a fifteen-minute breakfast or a ten-minute phone conversation that you can with a whole evening in which you both just watch television and say very little. If you are a parent, you've probably read about quality time; it's not only how much time you spend with your children but the quality of attention you give to them during that time that counts. The same is true of other relationships, including your marriage.

> "Carol always claimed I was guilty of this," Bob said. "Work used to be my Number One priority, even though I loved Carol. I also had family and social obligations that I felt I couldn't drop. But when we got back together, we both decided that the relationship had to come before everything else. I gave up a lot of outside activities that had just accumulated. Now we schedule regular time together when we'll sit down and talk, or go out and do something we like. Sometimes we'll just talk on the phone, especially when one or both of us is working late. It gives us a chance to catch up on each other's day and feel close—it's a good investment of time."

SIX: Develop a Support System That's Rooting for the Relationship

During the separation, you leaned heavily on your support system. You spent long nights talking to friends, and doing things with them to keep busy. Those support systems were vital to your survival and still are. Don't give them up now that you and your partner are back together. But be careful that you have the right type of support system. Old friends may be feeling neglected now that you no longer need them or believe you're making a mistake to reconcile. Some might even be jealous of your newfound happiness, especially if they are not in a good relationship of their own. Whatever the reason, these people can sabotage the relationship you are working so hard at. Talk with them. Make it clear that you are fully committed and that you could use their support. Focus on friends who truly want you to succeed.

> "My best friend, Fay, was there for me all during the separation," Carol said. "She cried with me, held my hand, listened to me for hours. When Tom and I got back together, she encouraged me every step of the way and seemed truly happy for me. But

Tom's friend, Hal, was just the opposite. He made it very clear that he thought Tom was making a mistake coming home. Tom likes Hal, but rarely sees him any more. We don't need the extra tension in our marriage at this stage. We want to be with friends who are rooting *for* us."

SEVEN: Keep Learning and Growing

Did you haunt the libraries and bookstores during your separation? Most separated partners search for ways to understand what happened to destroy their relationship. Reading helped you analyze your feelings and your relationship. Now that the two of you are back together, you haven't stopped needing information about yourself and what's happening between you. You still can benefit from suggestions on how to resolve problems, old or new, and strengthen your relationship. If you can take just one strong idea or one good suggestion from each book you read, you will continue to grow and build a stronger foundation. At the back of this book is a list of suggested readings. You and your partner might enjoy going through several of the selections together.

"As a matter of fact, I got the idea to go to counseling from a book I read," Tom said. "A friend of mine gave it to me. I had always thought that counseling was for really sick people; that healthy people should be able to solve their own problems. Reading the book gave me some practical ideas I could use right away. It also made me see how important it was that I understand myself if I wanted to understand someone else. Now that Carol and I are reconciled, we're reading books together, and Carol has started going to counseling with me."

EIGHT: Remember and Share the Love

Just as no one is a mind reader when it comes to problems in a relationship, no one is a mind reader for the good points, either. If you love your partner, let him know it. Every day, remind both yourself and your partner of the love between you. Serve up a compliment first thing in the morning. Think how happy your partner will be to wake up and see your smiling face and hear, "I love you because . . ." That one compliment, that one reassurance, can set the tone for the whole day. Call your partner at work, or leave a loving message on the answering machine at home. Even the worst day brightens when you're reminded of how much you're loved.

"I never used to be very verbal," Tom said. "I thought that Carol would just know how much I loved her. But one of the books I read said that it's important to say the words. Now I make a point of saying 'I love you, you mean everything to me.' I want Carol to know how much I value our relationship; and I really appreciate it when she tells me how important it is to her, too."

NINE: Cherish And Appreciate
What You Have Worked So Hard to Get

Many times you asked yourself, "Is this relationship worth the struggle?" Obviously, you answered *yes*, even though you might have had a few *yes, but*s . . . in there once in a while. When the new relationship isn't quite as good as you imagined, when he still hurts your feelings or is thoughtless, remind yourself of why you worked so hard at getting back together. What were your reasons? Just what is it about the relationship that made you go through everything you did in order to salvage the love?

Think about the good things that are happening to you right now. What nice things is your partner doing for you every day? What has he said or done lately that shows he loves and cherishes you? It's very easy to focus on how hard *you* are trying and over-look or take for granted your *partner's* efforts. When you notice something nice your partner does for you, comment on it! Everyone needs to be appreciated. You can do something as direct as saying, "Honey, I noticed that you bit your tongue when I talked on and on about my friend, even though that annoys you. Thank you very much for your patience. I love that about you."

You let your partner know that you recognize what he is doing, and remind him once more that you love him.

> "You'd better believe that I compliment Tom on his new communication skills, every chance I get!" Carol exclaimed. "I tell him every day how much I look forward to his coming home and talking to me, and how I think he's great for putting so much effort into it. The more I compliment him, the more he tries and the better it is for both of us. I keep indirectly reassuring myself too, with each compliment, saying that he loves me enough to make this effort. It's a good way of counting my blessings."

TEN: Anticipate the Good Times to Come

Once you have reminded yourself of your love, focus on the future. Think about the good times that lie ahead. Think about next week, next year, five years from now. What do you look forward to sharing with your partner? Are you looking forward to retirement and time to travel around the country? Do you dream of having a child, and seeing her grow into a happy, healthy adult? You put a lot into this relationship; what do you expect to get out of it? What do you fantasize about in those quiet moments when it's just the two of you together?

> "The night I proposed to Carol, we talked about our future together," Tom said. "We saw ourselves in a small town, raising our children. In the middle of all our problems, while we were separated, I felt very sad that we weren't going to have that dream. Now that we are back together, we talk about it even more. It's something we share, something we can work toward. It makes us closer together, having a common goal."

ELEVEN: Develop Tolerance

When couples live together in loving relationships, they can lovingly accept otherwise annoying habits because they are part of their partner's total personality. Couples who get back together said, "Be tolerant. Be forgiving. Have patience. Especially, be tolerant." You have both been through a lot. You both want your relationship to become even stronger in the future. Yet there will be setbacks along the way. When you recognize them, accept them as pauses, not full stops. Your attitude is all-important. If you demand perfection, you are going to be disappointed. We're all human—we all make mistakes; we all do things our own way. If you expect a few things to go wrong or your partner to have a few habits that annoy you, you can accept them and move on. The key is tolerance. Accept your own and your partner's foibles and focus on the positive.

TWELVE: Be Friends

Think of your partner as your best friend and treat each other accordingly. Consider how you act with the other friends that you treasure. Treat your partner with the same courtesy, respect, and affection that you would your best friend. This is your lifelong companion. You and he will spend more time with each other than with anyone else. You will know each other in more ways than anyone else—companions in the adventure called life. At the end, what will be important is how well you've expressed your love, how much you've shared of yourselves, and how good a friend you were along the way.

Your relationship has survived separation, and now you're back together again. You made the effort to put the pieces back together, and you're willing to continue to work to make your relationship strong. You're aware that a relationship is a product of the two of you, and you're willing to nurture it so that it will be mutually satisfying. With that attitude, and the tools you've acquired, you've got everything going for you. Keep your vision of reconciliation in front of you and know that it is achievable.

CHAPTER ELEVEN

Making a Lifetime Commitment:
What Successfully Reunited Couples Said

Winter Is Over
The emotional icicles grew and grew.
I wanted her to go . . . she did.
And so began a long, painful, lonely, eternity.
Time passed.
Then she called and said, "I don't need you anymore,
So let's be together . . . . I accept you as you are."
So, here we are . . . together.
Living and loving, learning and growing . . .
Knowing who we are, and what we want.
Finally at peace,
 With ourselves, and with each other.
My dearest Jeannie, love of my life,
Winter is over.

by *Lee Shapiro* (a poem to his wife)

After 22 Years Of Marriage . . .

Larry and Janice
Larry and Janice are typical of couples who had a deep underlying love for each other, but whose relationship was so dysfunctional that it seemed the only solution was separation. Coming

from alcoholic and emotionally abusive homes, they continually
struggled with issues of trust, dependency, fidelity, and control.

"I was the biggest victim that ever lived," Janice said. "But
after twenty-two years of marriage, I decided to do something
about it. I told Larry I was going to leave him in California and go
back to Kansas City to find out who *I* really was. We stayed
friends through all the fights—Larry even helped me with the
move. Besides, inside, I knew we would get back together again.
But I also knew I had to leave so that things could change."

"I was lonely, confused, and angry when Janice left," Larry
said. "I had no intention of ever reuniting. In a few days, the first
of many girlfriends moved in (one of the things Janice and I had
argued about was my desire for an 'open marriage') and I in-
tended to file for divorce."

"I didn't think I could take care of myself," Janice said. "It
was a struggle at first, but within a few months I had an apartment, a good job, and a social life. My job had a lot of responsibility, and my boss loved me. I felt self-confident for the first
time in my life, and found out I really didn't *need* Larry. But I also
knew that Larry and I were meant to be together. In spite of
everything, we were still the best of friends, and he had never in-
itiated a divorce. About a year later, I called him up and told him
I wanted to come back."

"I was very glad Janice called," Larry said. "It caught me by
surprise—I was both very happy and very frightened. During
the time Janice was gone, I had learned not to be so judgmental,
so intolerant and impatient—and I gave up screwing around. I
felt we had something to work on now, because we had both
grown a lot."

"Nothing Is More Important than the Relationship!"
Larry was typical of reunited couples, who talked of a deep underlying bond, when he said, "We've always been best friends
and we enjoy being together. We can sit and read for hours on
end, and not say a word, just commune. What made our reunion
work when we got back together was that we decided nothing
was more important than our relationship!"

When couples are torn apart, each partner tends to blame the
other. If only *you* did or didn't do this or that, our relationship

would be OK. When couples separate, they have a chance to focus on their own needs and responsibilities. When they reunite successfully, there is a realization that there are really *three* entities in every relationship: "you," "me," and "the relationship." They recognize that if the relationship is to survive and grow, the emphasis needs to be on *all three*. There's an enormous difference between saying "this is what *you* should do to make our relationship better" and saying, "this is what *we* could do to improve things."

Every couple who successfully reunites places the *relationship* first!

"Building Instead of Destroying"

Barry and Darlene

> "Now we're building together instead of destroying together," Barry declared, as he and Darlene discussed the new life they had created after reconciliation. Watching their easy interaction, it was hard to believe the couple had once experienced so much pain.

When you're first separated, there is a tendency to think of the situation as temporary. You hope to reunite as soon as possible. Thinking about being apart for months seems a long time. That you might be separated for *years* before coming together again seems unthinkable. Barry and Darlene were separated for four years, during which time Barry was briefly married to someone else before reconciling with Darlene. Although during their marriage, drinking and drugs were a way of life for both, Darlene's turning point came when her beloved brother was killed in an accident. She started recovery from alcohol abuse, but Barry did not—he left, telling her to get on with her life so she wouldn't be "dragged down" by him.

> Darlene was devastated. Barry spiralled downward for three more years. Finally, he said, "I entered a rehabilitation program

because I realized I had two choices; I could die soon, or I could change." During this entire time, Darlene never gave up hope of reuniting with Barry: but when he left the rehabilitation program and contacted Darlene, telling her he had changed, and asking her to marry him again, she said, "Prove it!"

"Actions Speak Louder than Words"

Like many partners in addictive relationships, Darlene had been disappointed so many times by unkept promises that she wasn't willing to risk taking any more chances. She didn't want to hear promises; she wanted to see Barry's words actually borne out by his actions. So she told him what she wanted. "I want a 'decent' engagement ring to symbolize a new and enduring commitment, and I want to feel an attitude that shows I'm not being taken for granted anymore."

A year later, at Darlene's birthday party, Barry insisted she open his gift first. An engagement ring was inside—and as all the guests watched, Barry formally proposed to Darlene once more. He had settled his financial obligations, his new business was starting to prosper, and it looked as if they would even be able to buy a house soon. He had done what he had promised.

Making a Lifetime Commitment

When there have been long-term, major traumas, it's natural to continue to feel uncertainty for a while. During the first year, Darlene still had a lot of doubts. Barry had had so many problems that she wasn't sure he really could change permanently. Barry was aware of the difficulties. "I knew I had to be really sure I could make a lifetime commitment to myself, in order to commit to Darlene," he said. "During the time I was in the rehab, I made peace with myself—it was a key to staying sober and being able to commit myself to the relationship."

"We Listen to Each Other—Trust Can Be Mended!"

Barry also found out that when you really want something, you learn to listen. "We don't keep things in anymore," he continued; "we listen to each other and don't take each other for granted. I used to lie to cover up for using drugs. Now, I no longer feel a need to lie to Darlene about *anything.*" Darlene nodded in agreement, "I never have reason to doubt anymore—trust *can* be mended!"

Talking, Planning, and Working Together

Whatever the problems your relationship has experienced, the important thing to know is that it *can* get better. However troubled they have been, relationships can be healed. They can go from devastating and traumatic to loving and fulfilling.

> "We've made huge strides in the last few years," Darlene continued. "The romance is back again. We go out with friends, but we also make certain to take a day, or an evening a week, just for ourselves. We've put the fun back in our marriage. Before, we never did anything. Now we walk along the beach, we make plans, we talk about goals, and we actually work toward those goals together. We're talking, planning, and pulling together."

"Why We Decided to Reunite"

Jay and Peggy

Of all the traumas that couples face, infidelity is one of the most painful. It strikes at the very heart of our self-esteem and sense of ourselves as sexual beings. The shock of betrayal and broken trust is profound. Sometimes one partner is totally unaware of the other's infidelity.

"We had just come back from dinner when Peggy told me she was involved with someone else," Jay stated. A successful businessman, he'd thought he had a happy marriage and begged his wife to start marriage counseling. But when his wife refused to stop seeing the other man, he moved out. "I've been very lucky all my life," Jay said. "I was very successful, and well-known in the community. It was extremely painful to tell my family and friends that my marriage had 'failed.'"

"I was feeling a lot of hurt and anger," he continued, "But I loved our child and I decided to support Peggy in any way I could. When her new boyfriend turned out to have problems of his own, I arranged for her to get counseling. I still had hopes that we would get back together, although they were extremely slim. My goal was to get my life in order and move forward.

"Almost a year after we split up I got a call from Peggy. She wasn't happy with the man with whom she had been living, and it wasn't working out. During therapy, Peggy had been learning a lot about herself and what she needed, and she wanted to talk about the possibility of reconciling. We decided to start counseling together, but continued to live apart and not see anyone else. After two months, we decided to reunite."

Forgiveness and Commitment

Because the pain of infidelity is so great, it requires an enormous sacrifice of your inner resources to detach yourself from the pain and to forgive. There are also continuing fears of recurrence that take time and the development of trust to dissolve.

Jay stated it well when he said, "There's a tremendous amount of forgiveness that has to take place and commitment to what you're going to do. I had a lot of fears about whether Peggy would really put the family first, and there are still events that trigger bad feelings about what happened while we were separated."

"Communication is really the key," Jay said. "We sit down together and make plans: for us individually and as a family. One of the things that worked best for us was to go away for a whole weekend and set goals. We decided to make a map, so that we both know what our goals and expectations are. We make it a point to get together for lunch regularly to see how we're doing. We also make time for just the two of us to take walks on the beach, go on weekly dinner 'dates,' etc."

"Totally Committed Forever"

Mindy and Steve

In Mindy's case, things culminated during a one-year period in which her husband, Steve, lost his job and was unable to get another one while her new fashion accessory business zoomed to instant success. It was the final blow to a nineteen-year marriage that was already in severe difficulty. Steve had been demanding and verbally abusive for a long time; he was also involved in an affair. Mindy felt unhappy, downtrodden, and suffocated.

When she tried to divert herself by taking classes one night a week, Steve said that she was spending too much time away from him and threatened to leave. Although she promised not to take any more courses, inwardly she rebelled, and went off to a retreat. As he had threatened, Steve left. But both partners started to cry as Mindy told Steve, "It's no good, we've got to release each other."

"After Steve left, I was so happy and relieved," Mindy said. "I felt as if a ten-million-pound weight had been lifted off my shoulders. I went shopping, I talked on the phone for hours, I read in bed till 3:00 a.m.— all the things Steve had never allowed me to do. I thought, 'The world is so wonderful—why didn't I do this a long time ago?' It was a wonderful, incredible period. I lost fourteen pounds due to happiness! I didn't want to get back together again—it was the last thing I wanted! But at the same time, I was sad. I felt intense sorrow because I really loved Steve and he was still a part of me."

Ambiguity is natural. In almost every case, there are shifting boundaries between the partners as to who leaves and who is left, who wants to get back into the relationship and who isn't ready. This is especially true when a deep bond of love continues to exist.

"He Started to Share His Feelings"

Steve took me out for my 40th birthday. I had lost weight and wore a new outfit. He seemed to notice me for the first time and told me how beautiful I looked. We started seeing each other and having wonderful times. I was so happy that we could still be friends. After a few dates, Steve revealed that he had been seeing someone else while we were married—even while we were in counseling! He wanted me to know that he hadn't really been trying during our marriage, and for the first time, started to share his feelings with me. (He was seeing a psychologist, so I think that helped him talk.) I went crazy and told him, 'You have to decide whether you want her, or me!' That night, I knew we were going to try again."

"It's OK to Be Vulnerable"

"Since then, we've done a *lot* of talking together. Over the next few months we shared things that happened over the last twenty years. We went through layer after layer after layer—until we got to the core. I felt very insecure about the possibility of his going back to the other woman, but I've worked that through now. One of the most frightening things was that I had left the marriage, and found out I could make it, and now I was giving up that independence and becoming vulnerable. But I've learned that it's OK to be vulnerable."

"We Have Unconditional Love"

"We have a strong partnership now," Mindy said. "If I come home and he sees I'm tired, he doesn't expect dinner. He doesn't watch as many hours of sports on TV any more, either. I'm taking classes in the morning now instead of at night. We're spending time with each other and wanting to be with each other. We also give each other space to be alone; we don't smother each other. And we try not to make judgments about each other any more. We really have an *unconditional love* now. It's something I've always wanted—I just never dreamt I could have it with Steve!"

The Road to a Successful Reunion

Each couple is unique, yet in many ways the same. Their relationships, whether of two or twenty-four years, followed similar stages on their way through breakup and reconciliation. During the relationship there was disappointment, anger, fear, resentment, apathy, trauma. After the breakup the partners each experienced pain, doubt, anxiety, self-knowledge, growth. After reconciliation came renewal, vitality, commitment, partnership, love.

Seeking answers, each couple made their way through the rough terrain of separation or divorce. But although the events leading to the breakup and the external solutions differed, the results of successful reunions were the same. Self-examination and self-knowledge, development of a sense of identity and personal responsibility, led to the internal growth that allowed the partners to come back into revitalized relationships.

The confidence and self-identity these couples gained from struggling with difficult emotions made them confident enough to risk becoming vulnerable, and to explore their relationship honestly. Their hard-won self-knowledge enabled them to communicate openly with their partner. Most of all, they were able to place the focus of their attention on the *relationship*, and to make a commitment to that.

What Successfully Reunited Couples Want You to Know

Develop Your Sense of Identity

When we interviewed the couples whose stories you have read, they stressed over and over again that the most important point, to have a successful relationship, is to develop a sense of your own identity. Kim expressed it best when she said, "You have to feel good about yourself before others, including the people closest to you, will like you or respect you."

> "You have to take a real good look at *yourself*, and see where the problem is, and correct it in *yourself* first," Darlene said. "Don't lose your own sense of self. I loved Barry so much I relied on *him* for happiness, rather than myself. Believe in yourself—*anything* can happen if you truly want it!"
>
> "When I regained confidence, Robert became interested again." Kim said. "All the time I was afraid he was going to leave me, and I clung tighter, it only drove him further away. When he realized he wasn't the center of my life and that I had other interests, he wanted me."
>
> The wife of an extremely wealthy man said, "Find your own identity and sense of worth. Look for something *you're* interested in and *you* can accomplish. It's very degrading to beg for money and builds up resentment."

"Know who you are and what you want; and know who the other person is, and what they want—then work together," Cheryl stated. "That sounds very practical. But it's a very different kind of love than you have at the beginning when you add in practicality and treat your relationship as an investment. It's a life goal."

Commit Yourself to the Relationship

"Don't sell your relationship short—take the commitment seriously," Jay said. The bottom line is that no relationship is perfect—each has its own set of problems. So focus on your needs and communicate them to the other person."

"It's worth the effort—you get out of it what you put in it," Cheryl said. "We've put a lot in our relationship and the rewards are tremendous!"

Communicate

"Talk, communicate," Carol said. "Face the problem, you'll have to anyway—eventually."

"Now there's trust in the relationship," said Kim. "We communicate *before* things get out of hand."

Many ingredients make up a successful relationship. In addition to the obvious ones, there are others often overlooked which are necessary for a fulfilling relationship. Tolerance is perhaps one of the most important but little recognized ingredients in a mature relationship.

"The biggest thing that ruins relationships is having to be right and not knowing what you need in your life," said Larry.

Julie added, "You can't change people. You have to work around things that bother you. We all have little habits that irritate others."

"A lot fewer things bother me," said Katie. "There are very few things in life that are worth getting upset about."

Share the Responsibility

"Share the problems and learn to be involved *together*," Carol said. "Instead of blaming, say 'This is something we need to deal with together.' When both partners are working, sharing the responsibility for our home is important, too. Larry and Janice not only run their business together, but enjoy doing their shopping, cooking and cleaning jointly. Sunday mornings, Larry prides himself on his gourmet brunches. When you work together, chores can be fun!

Develop a Belief System

"If I didn't have my faith in God I wouldn't be here today, because He pulled me through more than one bad situation," said Darlene.

"God's not going to give you any more than you can handle," Carol said. "I believe that strongly."

Be Friends

A wonderful bonus of being in a deeply committed relationship is that you have a best friend as well as a partner.

"*Friendship* is the most important thing," Katie stated. "I don't think you can have a long-term love relationship without friendship. It's the added dimension of trust and acceptance."

Guidelines to Think Positively

"If you've having a bad day, then get through it. Tell yourself, 'Tomorrow will be better.'"

"Share the problems and get involved together."

"It could be that *one* partner puts in the major effort at reconciliation. That was true for us in the beginning, but it's not true anymore. I think we've switched positions. What's good in our relationship is that we take up each other's slack."

Would We Do It Again?

When couples were asked whether they would go through the reconciliation process again, they were unanimous in saying it was well worth it. The only thing most said they would do differently would be to wait longer to reconcile. Darlene spoke for all of them when she said, "Don't be in such a hurry to get together. Looking back, I should have stayed on my own a little longer."

Partners who have an underlying love can bridge almost any gap—as was shown in these case histories. As you go through the peaks and valleys of separation and reconciliation, remember that the reward at the end is reunion with the person you love. Keep your eye on that goal—others have accomplished it, and you can too. As Larry and Janice said, "If we hadn't gone through what we went through, we wouldn't be here today. Our marriage has never been better. We value it *because* we almost lost it."

Some separations were as short as two months, others as long as four years. Some partners had marriages or affairs in between the breakup and the reunion. A few had had a child with someone else. But regardless of the obstacles, where self-searching was combined with a deep bond of love, these partners were able to find their way back to a mutually loving relationship.

CHAPTER TWELVE

Breaking Up and Getting Back Together:
Bill And Christy's Story

Stage One: The Problems Mount

"When I look back, I can't believe how much things have changed." Christy's soft voice belied the intensity of her feelings as she recapitulated the events of the past year to her sister. "I thought for sure that Bill and I would never get back together again. We had been through so much, and we seemed to have so much going against us. It's a miracle that we're together."

Bill nodded in agreement. "I remember when we split up. I was drinking and spending money like it was going out of style. Our bills weren't getting paid, and I had to file for bankruptcy. I knew Christy had a hard time working and taking care of the house and the baby, but I didn't show her any consideration at all. I was really nasty to her and the baby—as if I was trying to get back at her for something and I didn't even know what. I kept promising her I would change, but I never did for more than a few days. Then I just slid back into the same routine all over again.

"Finally, I really lost it one night and Christy kicked me out. I felt as if I were going crazy—I couldn't sleep, I didn't know what to do. Fortunately, my boss saw what was going on, and insisted I get help. I'll always be grateful, because it really changed our lives."

Christy broke in, "I could see how much Bill was hurting, but I couldn't seem to reach him. I thought a lot of our problems stemmed from his relationship with his father, an alcoholic.

Every time his father called, he seemed to be able to make Bill feel guilty and worthless. No matter how much I told Bill I loved him and believed in him, it didn't seem to help. I was afraid I would end up in the same kind of marriage as his mother. Even though I was scared, I knew I had to do something."

Needs and Expectations

Whenever we enter a relationship, we carry certain needs and expectations with us. Christy and Bill had gotten married after graduating from high school. Both were eager to leave homes marked by constant arguing, tension, and conflict. Bill was a sensitive young man who was especially glad to get away from the demands and put-downs of his father. Nothing he did was ever good enough, no matter how hard he tried. Christy's quiet personality and common-sense approach to life seemed just what he needed.

The couple experienced some problems during their first few years of marriage, but no more than other couples they knew. It wasn't until the birth of their daughter, Tessy, that major difficulties started to surface. As with many couples in troubled relationships, the birth of a child was an added strain. Christy wanted to quit her job because she felt it was important that she stay home with Tessy during the first years of her life. Bill agreed that Christy should have the right to do so, but pointed out that her check made the payments on the furniture and the entertainment system they had bought for their home.

He also felt resentful that Tessy now seemed to claim so much of Christy's attention. The quiet times they had spent together, the long walks, the talks late at night—all these seemed to have vanished. It was as if Tessy had taken his place as the most important member of the family.

Bill's own emotionally deprived childhood did not prepare him for being a nurturing parent. He was short-tempered and irritable with Tessy. It was a major source of conflict between him and Christy—especially since Christy had promised herself that she would be the kind of loving mother to Tessy that her own mother had never been to her.

Most importantly, Bill was seeking to "relax" more and more by drinking and spending money on things they couldn't afford. When Christy confronted him, he would become belligerent and verbally abusive. The situation reached a crisis when Christy discovered that they would have to declare bankruptcy because of the extent to which Bill had been spending and overdrawing their checking account. When Bill dealt with the situation by going on a drinking spree, Christy decided to throw him out of the house.

Stage Two: Separation

"The night I told Bill to get out I wasn't sure what I was going to do, but I knew I had to do something. I just couldn't take it anymore. Our fights had escalated over the last three months to the point where it seemed we were screaming at each other every night. A lot of nights Bill wasn't coming home until two or three in the morning, and I was terrified that he had passed out somewhere or had gotten into an accident.

"It was affecting Tessy too. She was getting nervous and not sleeping well. When I took her to the babysitter, she would cry and hang on to me. I couldn't leave her alone with Bill because he was so irritable when he was drinking. I remembered how frightened I used to be when my parents fought, and I didn't want the same thing to happen to her.

"I was scared, too. It seemed like my worst nightmare had come true. I had always promised myself that my marriage would be different from my parents'. And here I was—going through the same thing.

"I really loved Bill. He could be so tender and considerate. I remember on our first date he brought me flowers. No one had ever done that before. We used to talk for hours about our dreams and what we wanted to have in our lives. I trusted him and admired him—he really seemed to know what he wanted."

Trying to Make It Alone

"The day after Bill left I was panic-stricken. I just didn't know how I was going to survive without him. I had depended on him for everything. It wasn't as if I didn't have a responsible job—I did. People relied on me at work. But in my private life, it was as if my brain turned off and I let Bill take over.

"Thank God I had my sister to talk to. We've always been very close, and she had gone through a similar situation in her own marriage a few years before. I think that for the first two or three weeks, I spent most of my time on the phone with her, or Tessy and I would go and spend the night at her house. She really helped me by listening and reassuring me that I could make it without Bill.

"Most of all she supported my decision to separate. I was feeling so guilty—thinking that maybe if I had been a better wife, Bill wouldn't have needed to drink. She helped me see that Bill's drinking was his problem, not mine. I'll always be grateful for that."

Stage Three: Preparation

"When I started to get on my feet again, I realized that I had never had a chance to find out what I could do. I was so focused on being a good wife to Bill and a good mother to Tessy that I had forgotten all about me. Bill kept calling and saying he wanted to come home again, but it just didn't feel right to me. I didn't want to repeat all the turmoil of those last few months, and I was afraid he would just go back to his old behavior again. I knew that if I was ever going to get any self-confidence, I was going to have to prove to myself that I could make it without him.

"I bought a lot of books on relationships and read everything I could get my hands on. I also joined a support group for a while. Some of the things I learned about myself really helped my self-confidence. Listening to other people's stories helped me put what was happening in perspective. I got a lot of good practical ideas from the group, like how to handle Bill's visits with Tessy.

"One of my friends mentioned that Al-Anon was for family members of alcoholics. I wasn't sure if Bill was an alcoholic, although his drinking certainly caused problems in our lives, so I didn't want to go at first. I'm glad that I did, because it helped me understand what was happening with Bill, and I let go of trying to fix him. It was a relief to be able to concentrate on taking care of myself and Tessy.

"What I found out I needed most in separating was just the time and space to get to know myself, to find out what kind of a person I was and what I really wanted. Even though it was tough being a single parent, with all the books I was reading and workshops I was taking, I felt I was growing by leaps and bounds. When Bill called I still felt a little guilty, especially because he couldn't see Tessy as much as he wanted to, but I was determined to prove that I could make it on my own."

What I Learned about Me—Christy

"Probably the most important thing I learned about myself was that I am a strong person and I do have what it takes to make it in this world. I never really knew that before, so I didn't have the self-confidence that I have now. I always thought that other people could handle things better or were smarter than me. Now I know that I can take care of problems that come up. I have a lot more self-esteem.

"I also found out that I enjoy learning new things. Right now I've got so many books I want to read, I can't buy any more until I finish what I have. One thing I've definitely decided is that I'm going back to college and finish getting my degree. I dropped out when Bill and I got married because I wanted more time with him, but I've regretted it—especially when I got passed over for promotions. I know it won't be easy to go back to school, but I'm going to start, even if it takes me a long time to finish.

"Another thing I've learned about myself is that I'm good with people. I thought I'd be too embarrassed to talk in those support groups, but I surprised myself. I got in touch with a lot of issues and feelings that had been buried for years and let them out. I was really proud of myself, especially when somebody came up after a meeting and said that hearing about my experiences had really helped her see what was happening in her own life.

"I also found out that I was a lot better organized than I ever thought I could be. Being a single parent means that you're always juggling your time. It seems that I never have time for myself except for the hour between when I put Tessy to sleep and when I collapse into my own bed. But I've learned to write everything down and make sure that the important things get taken care of.

"I've also learned to handle money a lot better. I used to be one of those impulse buyers—my money used to just dribble away. I still don't have a budget, but I've got a lot more control over where my money goes. It's a nice feeling to know that I can pay all my bills!

"I know it sounds strange to say so, but I'm really glad I had that time to myself. I don't think I'd be the person I am now if I didn't."

What I Learned about Me—Bill

"I guess I never really knew how much Christy and Tessy meant to me until the night Christy kicked me out. I knew I was out of control—I never let Christy know how much I was drinking—but even though I kept promising to change, I couldn't seem to do it.

"After I moved out, I went through a really bad time. I was so down on myself. I moved in with a buddy from work, and the two of us just partied all the time. I don't know how I managed to hang on to my job. Finally, one night I got so drunk I thought I was going to die. I thought about Christy and Tessy, and I knew I wanted to live. So I called up my brother and asked if I could stay with him and dry out."

Starting Recovery

"It was really rough the first few days. My brother and his wife were there with me every minute. They took me to my first Alcoholics Anonymous meeting—I would never admit that I was an alcoholic before. It wasn't easy working on the AA program. There were things I had a lot of problems with, like learning to give up the need to control. I still have problems with that one. But I'm working on it. Christy can tell you that I'm making progress.

"What I also realized was that even though I hated the way my father treated my mother and us kids, I was doing the same thing to Christy and Tessy. He always found fault with everything—nobody could ever please him. And he always put us down. One thing I've learned is that I probably won't ever get the love I want from him, and I just have to learn to accept that.

"The Adult Children of Alcoholics group that I'm going to has helped a lot there. It's made me realize just how much of my thinking and the way I used to act was shaped by growing up in an alcoholic household. I didn't know what normalcy was. In a way, it's like being reborn. I'm starting all over again, and it feels great!

"Something else I've discovered is how I tend to sabotage myself. I know I'm smart, but whenever I get into a situation that's really good, whether it's at work or with Christy, I seem to mess it up. I don't know whether it's because my father always said I'd never amount to anything, or whether it's me, but I'm aware of it now. "

"I Can Change."

"Probably the most important thing I've found out is that I can change. When I lost Christy and Tessy my world fell apart. I knew I wanted to get them back and be a family again, and I was determined to do whatever it took. Christy didn't believe me at first—I know she was afraid I'd slip into the old habits. But I was determined to prove to her that things were different, that *I* was different."

Stage Four: Reconciliation

Why I Agreed to Get Back Together—Christy

"It's true that I had a hard time believing that Bill had really changed. We had been through so much together, and he had made so many promises that he had broken. I told him that I'd belive him if he proved it to me with his actions—and he did. "

Changes in Parenting

"One of the things that used to bother me about Bill was how he treated Tessy. He would be really rough with her and yell at her, so that even though she loved him and wanted his attention, she was scared of him, too. Now, he's a lot better. He plays with her when he gets home, and he's much more patient."

Changes in Finances

"Another problem we had was our finances. I know I was to blame too, but it seemed that whenever Bill got upset he would go out and buy himself a new toy that we couldn't afford. A lot of times it would be after an argument and he would say it was for me—but it just put us deeper in debt. Before Bill moved back, I insisted that we work out a budget and contacted all the creditors. Now, I handle the money because we both agree that I'm better at it. We have a business meeting once a month to see how we're doing, and we've actually been able to start a savings account. "

Changes in Attitude

"Probably the biggest reason was the change in Bill's attitude. We're friends now, and we respect each other. Instead of putting me down he supports me in what I'm trying to do and I do the same for him. We talk things out instead of arguing."

My Changes—Christy

"I had to go through my changes too. I knew it was important, if we were going to make it, for me to establish who I was and develop confidence in myself. I was unsure of Bill, but I was also unsure of myself. I needed to prove to myself that I could be self-sufficient, and not have to rely on Bill to take care of me. Our whole relationship is so much better now—we're really partners in life!"

"There wasn't any one reason that I decided to get back with Bill. It was a whole lot of things that made me change my mind. Most important maybe is that I learned I could trust him to do what he said he would do. I saw how different he was with Tessy, he stopped drinking, we got our finances together, and we really started to communicate with each other. When we have a problem we sit down and talk about it. We're each other's best friends now, and I feel that whatever comes up, we can handle it. "

"What We Want and Need Now"

"I used to think that if Bill really loved me he would satisfy all my needs, " Christy said, "and I used to blame him when he didn't. I know now that's not true. One thing I definitely learned during our separation was that I'm basically responsible for my own happiness."

"That's a big relief to me," Bill broke in. "When Christy expected me to know what she wanted without telling me, I felt a lot of pressure. I was never really sure how she'd react. Sometimes I'd do something thinking she'd like it, and she'd blow up because it wasn't what she wanted. Then I'd get mad and decide I wouldn't do *anything*. The fact that we're communicating so much better now means that I don't have to guess about things. I *know* what's important to Christy."

"One of my biggest needs now," Christy added, "is to finish my schooling. I want to get my degree so that I'm qualified to move up into management. It's going to take a while, and I'll need Bill's help, but it's something I'm determined to do. Fortunately," Christy smiled, "Bill thinks it's just as important as I do."

Christy and Bill's story illustrates how breaking up and getting back together again completes a cycle. Marriage is often based on a combination of infatuation and need. If all goes well, the needs are mostly filled, and infatuation turns into mature love. However, when the infatuation fades and your needs are unfulfilled, you become disappointed, resentful, and angry. This leads to frustrating attempts to get your partner to meet your expectations. And when you fail, the stresses that lead to a breakup begin to accumulate.

When separation seems the only solution, you are faced with a crisis situation that brings great pain, but also offers an opportunity for growth and renewal. As Bill and Christy found out, being on their own forced them to look at themselves in new ways and find new solutions to their problems. When they did, they were able to come back together, in a way that brought them the happiness and love they so greatly desired.

Right now, you may be wanting your partner back so much that the idea that you could take the time to work on yourself first seems impossible. But it *is* possible. Like the couples interviewed for this book who have successfully reconciled, your perspective will change, as you begin to discover your own strengths and resources. Build on your strengths and remember why you are working on yourself—it's to give you the best possible opportunity for the strong, loving, wonderful relationship you deserve to have.

How To Find A Therapist

You can find a therapist in several ways. Ask friends who have been through counseling to give you the names of those who have helped them. Look in the Yellow Pages under "Psychologists," "Marriage and Family Counselors," or "Clinical Social Workers," or "Psychiatric Social Workers." Your Employee Assistance Program, counseling referral service, church, or synagogue—all can give you the names of qualified professionals. Concerns about cost shouldn't keep you from getting help. Health insurance policies usually cover psychological services, but check your policy (if in doubt, call your agent and ask him or her directly). Universities and colleges often have psychiatric or psychology departments that run counseling centers at very low cost, as do YMCAs and other community agencies. Many therapists work on a sliding fee scale. Counseling comes in all price ranges, and many counselors will be willing to work with you.

In their book, *Love Fitness*, Harold Bloomfield and Sirah Vettese give some excellent guidelines for choosing a therapist. Among them are:

- Is he or she a licensed psychotherapist who is respected by the professional community and general public?

- Does the therapist have a pleasant disposition, a sense of humor, and appear to be functioning well in his or her own personal life?

- Do you feel safe, comfortable and at ease with the therapist?

- Is the therapist willing to explain his or her approach to your problem, as well as goals and probable length of treatment?

In addition to assisting you through the current crisis, a good therapist will also help you learn new skills that you can continue to use in the future.

Relaxation Exercises

30-Second Instant Relaxer

Sit comfortably, both feet on the floor, hands loosely in your lap.
Take a deep breath.
Let your jaw relax open, and exhale with a deep sigh.
Take another deep breath.
Let your jaw relax open, and exhale with a deep sigh.
Take another deep breath.
Let your jaw relax open, and exhale with a deep sigh.

Deep Muscle Relaxation

Sit comfortably, both feet on the floor, hands loosely in your lap.
Take a deep breath and clench your fists as tightly as you can.
Hold to the count of five—then exhale and relax your hands.
Notice how your hands feel when they're relaxed.
Take another deep breath and tighten up your face.
Tighten your nose and mouth and forehead as much as you can.
Hold to the count of five—then exhale and relax your face and jaw.
Notice the difference.

Take another deep breath and tighten your stomach and
  buttocks—get them as tight as you can.
Hold to the count of five—then exhale and relax.
Take another deep breath and tighten your legs.
Tighten and press them close them together as close as you can.
Hold to the count of five—then exhale and relax.
Take another deep breath and tighten your feet and ankles.
Hold to the count of five—then exhale and relax.
Now, take another deep breath and tighten your entire
  body; make it as rigid and stiff as you can.
Hold to the count of five—then exhale deeply and relax
  your body.
Let it sink into the chair and notice the difference when
  your body is completely relaxed.

Visualization for Relaxation

In visualization, you use your imagination to put yourself into a
pleasant, relaxed state. It's especially good to do before going to
sleep at night after you've done a deep-muscle relaxation exercise
such as the one above. Here are some visualizations you can use
to calm your mind and release stress.

Do the 30 Second "Instant Relaxer" or Deep Muscle Relaxation before doing this.

Imagine you are in a beautiful, relaxing place. It can be a
beach, the mountains, a green meadow, or any other place that is
restful for you. Imagine it in every detail. Look around and notice
the colors in your surroundings, the air on your skin, the warmth
of the sun, the sounds, and the odors. Make it as real as possible,
and linger as long as long as you like.

Imagine that you are in a fantasy spot—someplace that you
imagine as being perfect in every way. Imagine all the details
such as people, buildings, animals, sounds, and motion that
make your fantasy spot ideal. It may be a place you've always
wanted to visit, it may be an experience you've always wished

for, like being on a yacht or some romantic island—whatever you can imagine that really satisfies you.

Imagine a special place where you always feel peaceful, safe and comfortable—and where there is a special friend you can talk to who understands you. This can be a real place or an imaginary place; perhaps your grandmother's home with the smell of cinnamon rolls baking in the oven, or a special hiding place that only you know about, where you feel safe. Imagine yourself talking to your special friend and telling him or her all your problems. You friend is very wise and, as you talk, imagine your tensions dissolving away.

Suggested Reading

Dealing with Separation

Coming Apart, Daphne Rose Kingma. Ballantine Books, New York, 1987.

Crazy Time, Abigail Trafford. Bantam Books, New York, 1984.

How to Survive the Loss of a Love, Melba Colgrove, Ph. D., Harold I I. Bloomfield, M.D. and Peter McWilliams. Bantam Books, New York, 1976.

Journey Through Divorce: Five Stages Toward Recovery, M.D. Rosenstock, Judith Rosenstock, and Janet Weiner. Insight Books, New York, 1988.

Love Is Letting Go of Fear, Gerald Jampolsky. Nightingale-Conant, Chicago, 1987.

Rebuilding When Your Relationship Ends, Bruce Fisher. Impact Publishers, San Luis Obispo, California, 1981.

Successful Women, Angry Men, Bebe Moore Campbell. Random House, New York, 1986.

Recognizing Addictive Relationships

Codependent No More, Melody Beattie. Harper/Hazelden, New York, 1987.

Is It Love or Is It Addiction? Brenda Schaeffer. Harper/Hazelden, New York, 1987.

Love Is Never Enough, Aaron T. Beck, M.D. Harper & Row, New York, 1988.

Rebuilding When Your Relationship Ends, Bruce Fisher. Impact Publishers, San Luis Obispo, California.

The Struggle for Intimacy, Janet G. Woititz. Health Communications, Inc., Deerfield Beach, Florida, 1985.

The Cinderella Complex, Collette Dowling. Pocket Books, New York, 1981.

Women Who Love, Women Men Leave, Steven Carter and Julia Sokol. New American Library, New York, 1987.

Women Who Love Too Much, Robin Norwood. Pocket Books, New York, 1985.

Developing a Sense of Identity and Positive Attitude

The Assertive Woman, Stanley Phelps, M.S.W., and Nancy Austin, M.B.A. Impact Publishers, San Luis Obispo, 1975.

Codependent No More, Melody Beattie. Harper/Hazelden, New York, 1987.

Do I Have to Give Up Me to Be Loved by You? Jordan Paul, Ph. D., and Margaret Paul, Ph. D. CompCare Publishers, Minneapolis, Minnesota, 1983.

Intimate Connections, David D. Burns, M.D. New American Library, New York, 1985.

The Seven Principles of Highly Effective People, Stephen R. Covey. Simon & Schuster, New York, 1990.

Communication

The Assertive Woman, Stanley Phelps, M.S.W., and Nancy Austin, M.B.A. Impact Publishers, San Luis Obispo, 1975.

A Couple's Guide to Communication, John Gottman, Cliff Notarious, John Gonso, and Howard Markman. Research Press, Champaign, Illinois, 1976.

Lifemates, Harold Bloomfield, M.D., and Sirah Vettese, Ph. D. New American Library, New York, 1989.

Love Is Never Enough, Aaron T. Beck, M.D. Harper & Row, New York, 1988.

Marriage is for Loving, Muriel James. Addison-Wesley, Reading, Massachusetts, 1979.

Messages: The Communication Skills Book, Matthew McKay, Ph. D., Martha Davis, Ph. D., and Patrick Fanning, Ph. D. New Harbinger, Oakland, California, 1983.

Creating a Loving Relationship: Growth and Intimacy

Beyond the Power Struggle, Susan M. Campbell, Ph. D. Impact Publishers, San Luis Obispo, California, 1988.

A Conscious Person's Guide to Relationships, Ken Keyes, Jr. Love Line Books, Coos Bay, Oregon, 1986.

From Conflict to Caring, Paul Jordan, Ph. D., and Margaret Jordan, Ph. D., CompCare Publishers, 1989.

Getting the Love You Want, by Harville Hendrix, Ph. D. Henry Holt & Co., New York, 1988.

Learning to Love Forever, Adelaide Bry. Macmillan Publishing Co., New York, 1982.

Lifemates, Harold Bloomfield, M.D., and Sirah Vettese, Ph. D. New American Library, New York, 1989.

Marriage is for Loving, Muriel James. Addison-Wesley, Reading, Massachusetts, 1979.

The Couple's Journey, by Susan M. Campbell, Ph. D. Impact Publishers, San Luis Obispo, 1980.

The Road Less Traveled, M. Scott Peck, M.D. Touchstone / Simon & Schuster, New York, 1978.

When a Man Loves a Woman, Claude Steiner. Grove Press, New York, 1986.

Healing the Family Unit

Bradshaw on: The Family, John Bradshaw. Health Communications, Inc., Deerfield, Florida, 1988.

Helping Your Teenager Deal with Stress, Bettie B. Youngs. Tarcher/St. Martins, New York, 1988.

The Six Vital Ingredients of Self-Esteem: How to Develop Them in Your Children, Bettie B. Youngs, Ph. D., Learning Tools, San Diego, California, 1990.

Stress in Children: How to Recognize, Avoid and Overcome It, Bettie B. Youngs. Avon, New York, 1988.

A Stress Management Guide for Young People, Bettie B. Youngs, Learning Tools, San Diego, California, 1988.

More Tools for Achieving Reconciliation

How to Get Your Lover Back, by Blase Harris, M.D. Dell, New York, 1989.

Relaxation

Relax: How You Can Feel Better, Reduce Stress, and Overcome Tension, John White and James Fadiman, editors. Dell, New York, 1976.

Relaxation Dynamics, Jonathan C. Smith. Research Press, Champaign, Illinois, 1985.

Stress Management: A Comprehensive Guide to Wellness, Edward A. Charlesworth, Ph. D., and Ronald G. Nathan, Ph. D. Ballantine Books, New York.

Spirituality

Gift from the Sea, Anne Morrow Lindbergh. Vintage Books edition, Random House, New York, 1978.

Jonathan Livingston Seagull, Richard Bach. Avon Books, New York, 1970.

Power through Constructive Thinking, Emmett Fox. Harper & Row, New York, 1940.

The Prophet, Kahlil Gibran. Alfred A. Knopf, New York, 1960.

The Road Less Traveled, M. Scott Peck, M.D. Touchstone/Simon & Schuster, New York, 1978.

Children's Books on Divorce

Daddy Doesn't Live Here Any More, Betty Boegehold. Golden Books, New York, 1988.

The Boys and Girls Book about Divorce, Richard Gardner. Bantam Books, New York, 1971.

The Kids' Book of Divorce, Eric Rofes, editor. Random House, New York, 1982.

About The Authors

Bettie B. Youngs, Ph.D. is an internationally known lecturer, author, counselor, trainer, and consultant, and a frequent guest on radio and television talk shows. Her work has spanned more than 60 countries for nearly two decades, earning her a reputation as a respected authority in the field of personal effectiveness. She has won national acclaim for her work on the effects of stress on health, wellness, and productivity for both adults and children, and for her work on the role of self-esteem as it detracts from or empowers vitality, achievement and peak performance.

Bettie, a former professor at San Diego State University, and Executive Director of the Phoenix Foundation, is the author of a number of books, including *Stress in Children* (which has now been published in seven languages); *Helping Your Teenager: A Parent's Guide to the Adolescent Years*; *Is Your 'Net' Working? A Guide to Building Contacts and Career Visibility*; *Friendship Is Forever, Isn't It?*; and *The 6 Vital Ingredients of Self-Esteem*.

Bettie is a member of the National Speakers Association, and serves on the Board of Directors of the National Self-Esteem Council. She addresses audiences throughout the U.S. and abroad, meeting with nearly 250,000 young people and adults each year. She is married, the mother of a teenage daughter; and lives in San Diego, California.

Masa Goetz, Ph.D. is a clinical psychologist in private practice in San Diego, California, specializing in marriage, family, and child counseling. Dr. Goetz is a member of the California State Psychological Association, the California Association of Marriage and Family Therapists, and the Academy of San Diego Psychologists. She is a member of the Advisory of Families Against Drugs.

Masa works with a wide variety of clients in both her private practice and as a consultant with community agencies. She frequently conducts workshops and seminars and has extensive experience helping couples to resolve marital problems, deal with the stress of separation or divorce, or work their way back into their relationship.

Masa is the author of a number of audiocassette tapes including: *Visualization: A Healing Process; Visualization: Understanding Your Mental Images; Relaxation for Young People;* and *Relaxation for Children.*

Why Men Commit
Susan Curtin Kelley
$6.95, 188 pages, ISBN 1-55850-159-2
Trade paperback

Why does a man decide to commit to a relationship?

In *Why Men Commit*, Susan Kelley reveals the intriguing results of her extensive nationwide survey about why men choose a particular mate. She shows what men seek in a lifetime partner (it's not a great body), and how they change perspective when approaching marriage for the second time.

Men don't marry for the reasons most women think they do, and it is the women who understand this, the ones who know how to approach the issue of commitment with a man, who achieve enriching lifelong relationships.

- What do men think about long-term relationships?
- What are the characteristics of a man who won't commit, no matter what?
- What should you say — and avoid saying — when you want to make a lasting commitment?

Available wherever books are sold.

HOW TO ORDER: If you cannot find these titles at your favorite retail outlet, you may order them directly from the publisher. BY PHONE: Call 1-800-872-5627 (in Massachusetts 781-767-8100). We accept Visa, Mastercard, and American Express. $4.50 will be added to your total order for shipping and handling. BY MAIL: Write out the full titles of the books you'd like to order and send payment, including $4.50 for shipping and handling, to: Adams Media Corporation, 260 Center Street, Holbrook, MA 02343. 30-day money-back guarantee.

30 Secrets of Happily Married Couples
Dr. Paul Coleman
$7.95, 188 pages, ISBN 1-55850-166-5
Trade paperback

Dr. Paul Coleman has studied hundreds of couples and discovered that the strongest and happiest marriages share 30 distinct traits. This book outlines these secrets of happily married couples, and provides real-life examples of how to use the techniques.

Happy couples know the importance of:
- Not always compromising
- Balancing Logic and emotion
- Knowing how and when to forgive
- Uncovering hidden agendas
- Knowing when to keep quiet, and when not to

You don't have to be unhappy in your marriage to wish it could be happier. You can have a committed, caring relationship but still be weary of the complacency, frustrated by a partner's personality quirks. Its better to change your relationship than try to change your partner, and this book shows you 30 proven ways to do just that.

Available wherever books are sold.

HOW TO ORDER: If you cannot find these titles at your favorite retail outlet, you may order them directly from the publisher. BY PHONE: Call 1-800-872-5627 (in Massachusetts 781-767-8100). We accept Visa, Mastercard, and American Express. $4.50 will be added to your total order for shipping and handling. BY MAIL: Write out the full titles of the books you'd like to order and send payment, including $4.50 for shipping and handling, to: Adams Media Corporation, 260 Center Street, Holbrook, MA 02343. 30-day money-back guarantee.

Why Men Stray, Why Men Stay
Susan Curtin Kelley
$8.95, 172 pages, ISBN 1-55850-634-9
Trade paperback

If you want your relationship to last in spite of the outside temptations, changing expectations, and just plain boredom that destroy many marriages and other long term relationships, you need to understand how men think and why they act the way they do.

Susan Kelley has interviewed hundreds of men on what makes them stay or stray. She shows that getting a man involved is only the first step in a long journey of compromise patience, and flexibility that can create the secure , fulfilling , long-lasting relationship you want.

In *Why Men Stay, Why Men Stray*, men get to say what's really going on in their minds, and once you know what men are really looking for as well as the warning signs that can signal trouble on the horizon, you'll know how to make sure that your relationship is one of the exceptional few that survive.

Whether your married or single, having trouble in your relationship, or just hoping to avoid it — or if you're just baffled by the way men act —this book is for you!

Available wherever books are sold.

HOW TO ORDER: If you cannot find these titles at your favorite retail outlet, you may order them directly from the publisher. BY PHONE: Call 1-800-872-5627 (in Massachusetts 781-767-8100). We accept Visa, Mastercard, and American Express. $4.50 will be added to your total order for shipping and handling. BY MAIL: Write out the full titles of the books you'd like to order and send payment, including $4.50 for shipping and handling, to: Adams Media Corporation, 260 Center Street, Holbrook, MA 02343. 30-day money-back guarantee.